WINTERTH

WINTERTHUR IN BLOOM

WINTER, SPRING, SUMMER, AUTUMN

HAROLD BRUCE

Photographs by Gottlieb and Hilda Hampfler

Foreword by Henry Francis du Pont
A History of the Gardens by C. Gordon Tyrrell

A WINTERTHUR BOOK

Publication of the 1986 edition of Winterthur in Bloom *was made possible in part through grants from the Marmot Foundation and the Friends of Winterthur.*

Acknowledgements

I dedicate this book to Louise Schaefer, whose friendship and constant regard have encouraged and sustained me for many years. Thanks are due also to many friends and colleagues for the parts they have played in shaping this book. To my friends Dick Ryan, James and Mary Deeney, Jan Welch, and Julia Morris, I am grateful for the material help and the immaterial but perhaps more important encouragement given me over the past two years. To John D. Morse, Head of the National Extension Program at Winterthur, I am indebted for the conception of the idea for this book and for a great deal of its execution, and to Mrs. Edward T. Mitchell, his editorial assistant, and Mrs. Geraldine Fortenbaugh, his secretary, for the myriad tasks involved in preparing the manuscript for publication. Two teachers of mine have been directly instrumental in the creation of this book: Dr. Charles W. Dunham of the Department of Horticulture at the University of Delaware who not only taught me much of the horticultural and botanical knowledge necessary in its creation, but also was kind enough to read the manuscript; and Dr. Edward H. Rosenberry, Chairman of the Department of English of the University of Delaware, who has guided and encouraged me for many years. To him also and to Dr. William C. Steere, Director of the New York Botanical Garden, and to C. Gordon Tyrrell, Director of the Winterthur Gardens, I am grateful for reading and commenting on the manuscript.

*Library of Congress Catalog Card Number: 68–15483
ISBN: 0-912724-01-3*

*Designed and produced by Chanticleer Press, New York
Printed and bound by Dai Nippon Printing Company, Tokyo, Japan
Second printing 1986*

Foreword

The history of the Winterthur gardens as written by Gordon Tyrrell is very complete. His account of their development and Harold Bruce's description of the plantings throughout the garden make me feel that my planting of thirty years ago has been successful. I like to see the shape and size of big shrubs; even though they are always part of a group, one has to know when planting just how big and tall the shrubs are going to be. I would mention the Chaenomeles Walk and the Sundial Garden as examples of this sort of planting. In his study of the garden Mr. Bruce very kindly illustrates what I have tried to accomplish through the years. My work is in the gardens; the story he has written leaves little for me to say except that I hope everyone will enjoy the book as much as I have.

HENRY FRANCIS DU PONT

Winterthur
July 1967

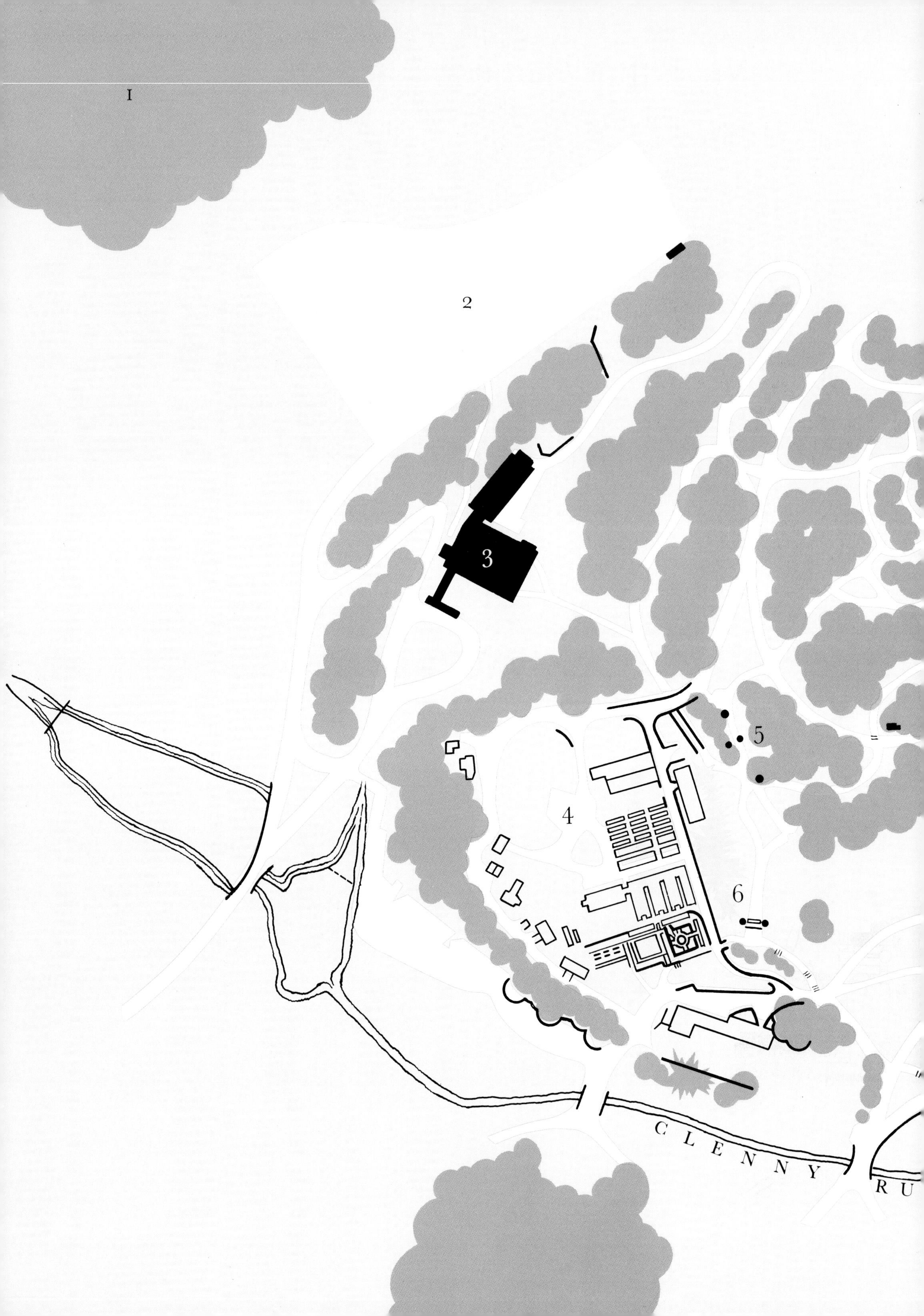

I

2

3

4

5

6

C L E N N Y

R U

Key to Winterthur Gardens

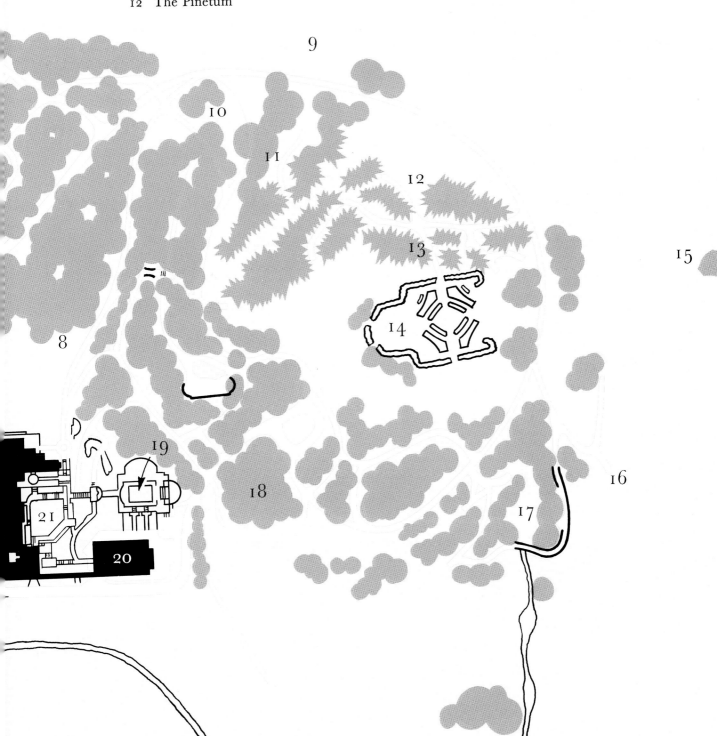

A History of the Gardens

BY C. GORDON TYRRELL

The Winterthur estate came into existence in 1839 when James Antoine Bidermann and his wife, Evelina Gabrielle, the daughter of E. I. du Pont de Nemours, built their home on the present site of the Museum, three miles northwest of Wilmington, Delaware. They named it Winterthur, after the town in Switzerland where Mr. Bidermann's family had lived. The Winterthur gardens, which today comprise about sixty of the estate's almost one thousand acres, had their origin in a sunken garden laid out by the Bidermanns near their new home. In 1902 Colonel Henry A. du Pont, a nephew of Mrs. Bidermann who had moved to the estate in 1875, enlarged and developed the sunken garden into terraces of perennials, roses, waterlilies, and flowering trees. The Louise du Pont Crowninshield Research Building now occupies this site.

Colonel du Pont's son, Henry Francis du Pont, the present owner of Winterthur, began naturalizing daffodils and other bulbs in front of the old house during the early 1900's. By 1910, grape-hyacinths, snowdrops, squills, chionodoxa, irises, daffodils, crocuses, adonis, and other small bulbs bloomed in the woodland between the house and the back drive. These have been increased each year until the planted area, known as the "March Walk," now extends from the house to the ancient saucer magnolia at the bend in the back drive.

Azaleas came to Winterthur at an early date. One of the first was the lovely *Rhododendron mucronatum* cv. 'Magnifica,' which is today perhaps the most widely used azalea cultivar in the whole garden. In 1915 Mr. du Pont obtained seventeen of the Kurume azaleas which the Japanese had exhibited at the San Francisco Exposition. These were propagated and were eventually planted by the hundreds in the woodland behind the house, along with many seedling rhododendrons purchased in the 1930's from Charles O. Dexter of Massachusetts. Today the area, known as the "Azalea Woods," is a great feature of Winterthur.

Another important feature of the gardens, the Pinetum, was laid out in 1914 by Colonel du Pont. More than fifty species and varieties of conifers were planted initially, the only additions being two trees of the recently discovered dawn redwood (*Metasequoia glyptostroboides*). All these trees, which include pines, spruces, hemlocks, firs, junipers, arborvitaes, Japanese umbrella-pines, and two magnificent blue atlas cedars (*Cedrus atlantica glauca*), are now fine, mature specimens.

Winter

Mr. du Pont's early association with such plantsmen as C. S. Sargent, E. H. Wilson, and Karl Sax of the Arnold Arboretum is responsible for the introduction of many choice trees and shrubs at Winterthur: buckeyes, tree peonies, azaleas and rhododendrons, honey-suckle, crab apples, mock-orange, lilacs, and cherries. Soon after their initial introduction to cultivation, Mr. du Pont obtained from these men plants which today are considered part and parcel of any good garden. In 1927, when Mr. du Pont took over the estate on the death of his father, he first developed the Pinetum area, where he began planting the Chaenomeles Walk and the hillside of viburnum. At this time work was also started on the group of early-flowering winter-hazel and *Rhododendron mucronulatum* which is known today as the "Corylopsis-Mucronulatum Walk."

The next era of the gardens' history coincides with the great addition to the house during the years 1929–31. This addition was necessary to accommodate Mr. du Pont's grow-ing collection of the decorative arts made in and imported to America during the seven-teenth, eighteenth, and nineteenth centuries, which in 1951 was opened to the public as The Henry Francis du Pont Winterthur Museum. During this period of construction, much work was done on the terraces and other features of the garden to the east of the present Museum building. On the site of the small pool below the terraces, a swimming pool was constructed, and in 1936 ornamental grillwork was used on top of the wall surrounding the new swimming pool.

In 1929 an iris garden had been laid out between the present Peony Steps and the cast-iron figures of George and Martha Washington. This was given up ten years later

9

Spring

when it became evident that iris enthusiasts were interested only in the newest varieties
of irises. After 1939 the area was planted with seedling Ghent azaleas. These remained
until 1946 when they were moved to their present location on the path to the White Gate;
in their place were put azaleas 'Magnifica' and 'Coral Bells,' which remain there today.
The Peony Garden did not come into existence until after 1953. Today it holds a fine
collection of Japanese, Chinese, and French hybrid peonies, with the dominant group
being both tree and herbaceous peonies of the Saunders strain.

Another display of early color was created in 1946 with the planting of two dozen
Rhododendron praevernum at the east end of the Azalea Woods. Other additions in 1946
included the Gable azaleas near the George and Martha Washington figures, the great
banks of azalea 'Hinodegiri' and Kaempferi hybrids south of the Sundial Garden, the
group of purple azaleas in front of the huge old Sycamore, and the many hybrid azaleas
along the walk from the Museum to the Sundial Garden.

About 1957–58 Mr. du Pont planned the areas of the Sundial Garden. Formal beds
around the sundial itself were designed by the landscape architect, Marian Coffin, who
had earlier worked on the fish pools and waterfalls below the east terrace of the Museum.
Immediate effect was achieved through the use of a great deal of fully mature plant material from other parts of the estate in addition to some fine new plants, such as the cherry
'Hally Jolivette' and the crab apple 'Henrietta Crosby.'

In the 1950's development of the hellebores along the Hellebore Walk was begun. Varieties of Christmas and Lenten-roses (or hellebores) and many other choice low-growing

Summer

plants were planted among the corylopsis and Korean rhododendrons to enhance this early display. Another area of the garden, known today as "Oak Hill," was also begun in the 1950's with a late display of color in mind. Many varieties of Glenn Dale azaleas, mock-orange, deutzia, spirea, and other June-blooming material were planted among the young oaks; in addition, a special grouping of native azaleas which bloom from May to August and provide a wide range of color, was begun. The planting was expanded in the early 1960's. In 1961 the Pavilion was completed to serve as a center for the Garden Tours.

Some plantings were started around the old Sycamore east of the Sundial Garden prior to 1960, but in that year began the serious development of a collection of late-blooming shrubs comparable to those on Oak Hill. Along three parallel paths, late azaleas, deutzias, mock-oranges, tamarisks, late magnolias, catalpas, golden-rain trees, Japanese dogwoods, and other late-blooming trees and shrubs were planted. Beds of lilies were laid among them. On the brink of a hill at the southern edge of the planting, the Bristol Summerhouse was erected, commanding a fine view of the valley through which Clenny Run flows. To the north of the Sycamore, a whole hillside was planted with many species of viburnums, interplanted with Kaempferi and Glenn Dale azaleas, and in 1962–63 the "Lookout," a structure of brick arches supporting a peaked tin roof surmounted by a leaded eagle with spread wings, was built. The roof of the Lookout was designed by Thomas T.Waterman, a member of the Historical American Buildings Survey who was architect at Winterthur from 1933 until 1950.

Near the foot of the valley south of the Sycamore area lies an abandoned quarry which

Autumn

in 1960 was planted with several species of Asiatic candelabra primulas. Several springs keep the base of the Quarry constantly wet, so bog plants such as the primulas thrive, and today they provide a great deal of color from early spring through summer. The natural rock outcropping along the wall of the Quarry was supplemented with rock brought from other parts of the estate. Many choice shrubs have been planted in the rockwork, which has now been extended along the little stream draining the Quarry. At the junction of this stream and Clenny Run a pond was dug in 1962. In the autumn of 1966, a larger pond was created farther down the meadow to insure an adequate supply of water for Winterthur's azaleas, shrubs, and trees. In 1963, after paths had been laid, Chandler Woods was opened to the public. This small acreage of native woods at the western border of the estate, including a fine bank of mountain-laurel, is now preserved for posterity as a nature walk.

Finally, a new grass walk has been made along the ridge halfway down Oak Hill, with a stone terrace which offers a fine view of the new *Primula japonica* bed in the meadow below. Along this walk are planted many fine summer-blooming plants such as late spireas, hawkweed, butterflyweed, indigo, genista, rose campions, heathers, heaths, and andromeda. These new additions to the Sycamore, Quarry, and Oak Hill areas present the visitor with an unbroken series of late-blooming plants from the time he leaves the Sundial Garden to the time he leaves Oak Hill. These recent plantings, plus those begun more than a century ago and altered now and then to suit changing conditions, demonstrate that the organic art of gardening is an art not only for all seasons, but for continuing time.

Winter

The gardens of Winterthur lie at the northern edge of what an ornithologist friend of mine calls the "mockingbird belt." They are located near Wilmington, Delaware, where the climate is dramatically variable, not only within each season but even within each day. There are winter days at Winterthur so dark that the early arrival of evening is scarcely noticed, and brilliant days made infinitely more brilliant by a coat of newly fallen snow. There are cold days when the earth remains firmly locked in frost; mild, wet days when every tree, shrub, and building drips constantly, when every depression becomes a pond and every ditch a gurgling stream, when the only sound is the sound of rushing water.

Winter in northern latitudes has a spare beauty. The lines of leafless trees form dark, delicate patterns against the pale sky; white snow glistens against bare trees, identifiable by shape and trunk color rather than by leaf. The colors of winter are subtle. A field of dead grass reveals countless shades of brown. Woodland sparrows are not drab, but chestnut, fawn, beige, rufous, and russet.

Winter refines our senses, preparing us for the glories of spring. In February, a tiny snowdrop seems as lovely as any of summer's roses; the unfolding of the spidery petals of witch-hazel on a January afternoon presents a minor miracle.

The ground at Winterthur is hardly thawed before the earliest of spring bulbs, the snowdrops, appear. Chaste and delicate, these most fragile of flowers bloom immaculate against the damp, dark earth and sodden leaves from which they spring. In south-facing pockets that catch the sun, they bloom in January, sometimes as early as New Year's Day.

Of the several species of snowdrops at Winterthur, the showiest is undoubtedly the giant snowdrop, *Galanthus Elwesii*. This native of Greece and Turkey, probably the finest snowdrop for eastern gardens, is for some reason seldom grown in America. It achieves on occasion a height of eighteen inches, and it is remarkable for its broad, glaucous leaves and its large, long-stemmed flowers of purest white, their inner segments strongly marked with green. Completely hardy and quick to increase, it is a splendid subject for naturalizing in woodlands and other semi-shaded areas.

All snowdrops prefer a half-shaded location, though they will also do well in deep shade

Giant Snowdrop.
Galanthus Elwesii

and in dry, sunny spots when a generous helping of peat or humus is worked into the soil before planting. Bone meal, because of its slow action, is the best fertilizer. Snowdrops, unlike daffodils and tulips, are best transplanted and divided immediately after flowering, taking care that the roots do not become dry. If transplanted later in the season, after their leaves have died down, they often take a season to reestablish themselves. Unfortunately, the bulbs are available from commercial sources only in the fall.

Galanthus is derived from the Greek for "milk" and "flower," an allusion to the white flowers of all the species in the genus. Snowdrops are members of the amaryllis family, *Amaryllidaceae*. As can be seen from the form of flower, leaf, and bulb, they are closely allied to the snowflakes *(Leucojum)* and the daffodils *(Narcissus)*.

Winterthur's March Walk is a sheet of color in late winter and early spring. Thousands of delicate mauve *Crocus Tomasinianus* bloom with golden yellow *Adonis amurensis* to produce a color combination which is the quintessence of oncoming spring. *Crocus Tomasinianus* is one of the earliest species crocuses, beginning to bloom with the snowdrops in February and early March. More slender, delicate, and refined than the common Dutch hybrid crocuses, "Tommies," as they are called in England, are not often seen in American gardens. This is a pity, for they are hardy, increase rapidly, and, coming almost a month before the hybrid crocuses, are a delight to the winter-weary eye.

The tiny corms of *Crocus Tomasinianus* may be purchased quite inexpensively from bulb dealers. Their culture is like that of other types of crocuses: they should be planted in the

Bank of Giant Snowdrops. *Galanthus Elwesii*

A Clenny Run Pond

fall, preferably not too late, three inches deep, in sun or shade. As with all spring-flowering bulbs, the foliage should be left intact until it withers in late May or early June, so that the corms develop sufficiently for the following year's bloom. *Crocus Tomasinianus* sows itself, spreads rapidly, and, once established, lasts indefinitely. It is hardy throughout most of the United States.

Unquestionably the brightest of the early flowers at Winterthur is the Amur adonis, *Adonis amurensis*. This small relative of buttercups and peonies, a native of Siberia, northern China, and Japan, opens its shiny, brilliant yellow cups before the snowdrops have faded, and continues to bloom with the early crocuses and squills. The flowers unfold as soon as the plants push through the ground, usually in February, and remain open through several weeks of inclement weather.

A. amurensis grows from a mass of cordlike roots and will therefore not bear long periods out of the ground, as true bulbs will. The best times for planting or dividing are in June, when the leaves are yellowing, or in the fall, when the plants are dormant. The plant produces a mound of lush, green, fernlike foliage, six to twelve inches high, and remains in good condition until it yellows and dies in June. It is quite rare in American gardens and deserves to be better known. Several distinct varieties, ranging in color from nearly white to orange red, have recently been imported from Japan and planted near the entrance to the Museum building.

Greek legend held that *A. annua,* a related species with blood red flowers, sprang from

"Tommies" and Amur Adonis on March Walk. *Crocus Tomasinianus* and *Adonis amurensis*

Crocus chrysanthus cv.
'E. P. Bowles'

the blood of the dying Adonis. *Adonis amurensis,* which takes its specific name from the Amur River in Siberia, is hardy throughout the United States.

Not all the plants on the March Walk are rare. Among the familiar faces here are the Dutch hybrid crocuses, which bloom later than the species crocuses and provide a kind of connecting link between the earliest bulbs and the later squills and daffodils. Everyone has crocuses. They are so familiar that we seldom realize how much beauty would be missing from early spring gardens if they did not exist. When skies are still heavy with snow clouds, and birds in the woods are still singing their brief winter songs, the first crocuses open their lacquered petals of yellow, purple, silvery mauve, pale lavender, and maroon—all striped and sanded, mottled and feathered with deeper colors—each with its brilliant orange stigma glowing in the dark throat of the flower. Delicate, yet large and colorful enough to make a show, these hardy hybrid crocuses amply repay the gardener in spring for the little money and labor spent putting them in during the fall.

Native to Mediterranean regions, crocuses are especially sensitive to sun. On drab days they remain tightly rolled, nearly colorless and quite unnoticeable. But at the first touch of the sun, the glistening petals quickly unfurl; the flower opens itself wide as though it were attempting to catch a maximum of warmth and light.

In addition to the Dutch hybrids, many species crocuses grow at Winterthur—the smaller snow crocuses that bloom before winter is over, such as *C. chrysanthus* and *C. Tomasinianus,* and species, *C. speciosus* and *C. zonatus,* which bloom in November. The genus is very large,

Amur Adonis. *Adonis amurensis*

Dutch Hybrid Crocuses

and contains some exquisite flowers. Crocus corms look like gladiolus corms in miniature. They should be planted early in the fall at a depth of about twice the height of the corm. Crocuses are able, however, to pull themselves down by means of retractile roots until they reach the depth they need.

Among the very early flowers on the March Walk is the earliest and rarest of the squills, *Scilla Tubergeniana,* which is distinguished by its large flowers, nearly an inch across, and its pale ice blue coloring. This plant is a relative newcomer to gardens. It was discovered several years ago in northwest Iran by a collector for the Dutch firm of Van Tubergen (hence the specific name), and not until recently has there been sufficient stock of the bulbs to permit widespread cultivation. Its lovely form and coloring make it one of the finest additions to the early garden. Members of the genus *Scilla* belong to the lily family, *Liliaceae.* They do well when planted in the autumn, three to four inches deep, in sun or shade. For naturalizing beneath shrubbery or in woodlands, they are superb. *Scilla* is the classical name for some members of this group, commonly called squills. Near relatives are tulips, stars-of-Bethlehem, trout-lilies, and hyacinths.

On the March Walk, the early *S. Tubergeniana, bifolia,* and *sibirica* mingle with blue chionodoxa, miniature daffodils, rue-anemones, and other spring flowers, creating wonderfully mixed, multicolored drifts of blossoms. *Scilla sibirica* stands out because of its intense Prussian blue color, which on a dark day seems to flash with a deep inner glow. The variety *atrocoerulea* is more robust than the species, and is usually known as 'Spring Beauty' in America.

Persian Squill.
Scilla Tubergeniana

Another interesting plant in this alliance is the Chinese squill, *S.chinensis*, which differs from the others in having pink or mauve-pink flowers, and in blooming in late August or early September. It is very hardy, and spreads quickly from self-sown seed. The best time to move it is in midsummer before the flowers show, for the plant is dormant at that time. A grassland plant in the wild, this species must have sun to perform well in the garden.

Blooming at the same time as *Scilla bifolia* and *S.sibirica* are the members of the closely related genus *Chionodoxa*, whose English common name is "glory-of-the-snow." Chionodoxas so closely resemble squills that it is difficult for the layman to distinguish between the two. The plants themselves apparently have the same difficulty, for they regularly crossbreed, producing the hybrid genus×*Chionoscilla*. At Winterthur, two species of *Chionodoxa*, the intense blue *C.sardensis* and the paler blue *C.Luciliae*, both from the mountains of Turkey, grow by the thousands on the March Walk, in the woodlands, and along paths all over the garden. Culture is the same as for *Scilla*. The name *Chionodoxa* is Greek, *chion* being the root for "snow," and *doxa* meaning "glory."

Little plants along the March Walk seem to stand still on cold days, then grow quickly during the milder spells. They are covered by successive snows, which harm them not at all. Such a plant is *Leucojum vernum*, the spring snowflake, which blooms in the snows of March. This native of Central Europe is one of the prettiest of the spring bulbs. With its deep green, grasslike leaves and nodding white flowers, it resembles *Galanthus* (snowdrops). The flowers of *Leucojum*, however, are larger than those of *Galanthus*, and have six segments,

Beeches, Oaks, Tulip-Poplars, and Snowdrops

Spring Snowflake. *Leucojum vernum*

all of equal length. In *Galanthus*, the inner three segments are much shorter, and are rolled into a sort of tube. Both plants have flowers of pure white, each "petal" tipped with a bright green or yellow spot.

Leucojum bulbs should be planted two to three inches deep in sun or shade. Like snow-drops, they do best when moved soon after flowering, rather than later in the season. They can be left undisturbed for years and will increase rapidly under good conditions. Preferring soils that retain plenty of moisture throughout the season, they seldom flourish in locations that bake dry during the summer. This preference for moisture is even more marked in another species, the larger summer snowflake *(L. aestivum)*, which has become naturalized in Delaware on the marshy banks of the Christina River south of Wilmington. *Leucojum* belongs to the amaryllis family, *Amaryllidaceae*. The generic name is a latinization of the Greek *leucoeion* meaning "white violet"; *vernum* is Latin for "of the spring," and *aestivum* for "of the summer."

A member of the large and distinguished buttercup family, the winter-aconite *(Eranthis hyemalis)* blooms in Delaware in March. At Winterthur it is naturalized in quantity on banks adjacent to the March Walk, where, along with crocuses, squills, adonises, snow-flakes, and snowdrops, it forms a multicolored carpet during early spring. Though less showy than its similar but larger relative, the adonis, *Eranthis hyemalis* has a charm all its own. The flower consists of petal-like sepals of clear yellow which form a cup an inch or two across. This cup is set in an involucre of glossy green encircling the flower like an Elizabethan ruff, all borne on a stalk little more than two inches tall. It is shown here blooming with the spring snowflake *(Leucojum vernum)*.

The winter-aconite is a native of Europe, and is hardy throughout the United States except in the extreme North. The plant grows not from a true bulb but from a tuber that is rather like a tiny, misshapen potato in appearance. Once established, it will flourish in

Winter-Aconite and Spring Snowflake. *Eranthis hyemalis* and *Leucojum vernum*

Beech Roots

any reasonably fertile and well drained soil. A woodland location suits it best, however, where it will spread rapidly from self-sown seed. Failure with the plant most often results from planting the tubers too late in the year. They should be obtained as early in the fall as possible—in September or even August—and planted immediately, for out of the ground they deteriorate rapidly. The foliage of winter-aconite, like that of all spring-flowering bulbs, dies down in June and does not reappear until the following spring.

One of the true bulbous irises, *Iris reticulata*, is native throughout much of the Near East, from Russia and the Caucasus to Persia and Turkey. In Delaware it begins blooming with the early crocuses in March. Its large, showy flowers, borne on stems only a few inches high, are of typical iris shape, having three upright petals, called the "standards," and three broader descending petals, each marked with a gold spot, called the "falls."

Iris reticulata is hardy throughout most of the United States. The small bulbs are easily obtainable from commercial sources and should be planted three inches deep in early fall. They do well in ordinary garden soil, in full sun or very light shade. Bone meal, applied at planting time, is the best and safest fertilizer. After flowering, the rushlike leaves will reach a foot or more in height before turning yellow and dying off in June. As with most spring bulbs, this foliage should remain uncut until it yellows; it must produce food to be stored in the bulb for the following season.

Of several color variants of this species, the typical form is a deep mauve. 'J. S. Dijt' is a deep wine or claret color; 'Cantab' is a pure sky blue; and 'Wentworth,' 'Harmony,'

Iris reticulata cv. 'Royal Blue'

Chinese Witch-Hazel
on Terrace.
Hamamelis mollis

and 'Royal Blue' (illustrated here) are shades of deep blue. All have the typical golden spot on the falls. The name iris, from the Greek goddess of the rainbow, is an allusion to the many beautiful colors found in this genus. The specific name *reticulata* refers to the covering of the bulb, which in this species appears netted or woven of coarse fibers.

For graceful form, no early flowers at Winterthur are more pleasing than *Iris reticulata*. They first appear among the snow and slush of March as fat, blue-green spears, then as fatter blue cylindrical buds, and finally as large flowers, with all the charm and intricacy of design found in the later, taller irises. Absolutely impervious to cold, they bloom on through the rough weather of late winter and early spring. A sunny morning after a snow-fall, when feathers of snow nestle in the center of each glowing blue and gold flower, is worth waiting for throughout the year.

Garden structures are essential in a large garden because they provide a constant note in a continually changing picture. The circular garden seat shown here is perhaps never so appealing as after a clinging, late winter snow. The simplicity of the conical roof contrasts with the gaunt angularity of the Osage-orange tree and the dense foliage of azaleas and evergreens, subdued now by the blanket of white. In spring the seat will not be changed, though the flamboyant colors of the azaleas will have transformed its surround-ings. (See page 106.) In summer it will remain the same, though deep in the shade of overhanging trees. In autumn it will appear still and unmoving while the whole face of the garden changes to red and gold, and falling leaves swirl in the winds of October.

The Quarry

And in early winter it will remain still unchanged, its spare symmetry contrasting with the harsher, irregular lines of the naked trees around it.

Another of the many faces of winter appears on the south-facing terrace of Mr. du Pont's house. The snow has gone, and a warm sun has caused the fragrant yellow blossoms of the Chinese witch-hazel *(Hamamelis mollis)* to open wide. Here the seasonal flowering and leafing of the witch-hazel introduces an element of change which contrasts strongly with the changeless aspect of the surrounding building. Even the shadow of the plant provides a delicately irregular tracery which moves daily across the uniform paving stones as the sun crosses the sky.

The Quarry, stripped of much of its summer greenery, seems a cold and forbidding place; the rocks seem to frown. After the first snowfall, however, the scene changes. The rocks are softened by their covering of white. Blue-green sprays of juniper and bronze-purple winter foliage of leucothoe and holly-grape gleam against the snow. In bare places, the tiny, dark rosettes of primrose and rock cress, each with a living bud at the center, wait for the spring.

The Museum area is perhaps loveliest in winter. The fine view of it shown here would be impossible at any other time of year: the great flight of steps leading down from the east terrace to the swimming pool with its grillwork gates and vine-covered bathhouses, the whole dusted with a light coating of snow.

The area is also rich in floral display during the winter, the plants around the building itself providing a succession of bloom throughout the year. The sweet flowers of vernal

View from East Terrace of Museum

Sasanqua Camellia.
C. Sasanqua

witch-hazel greet the new year at Winterthur. Snowdrops come just a little later. In February and March, crocuses and forms of *Iris reticulata* appear, and if the winter has been mild, a few gorgeous blooms may show on *Camellia japonica*. Slightly later, pasqueflowers and adonises appear. In late spring the dove-tree at the foot of the terrace will bloom, and, in summer, yellow and orange trumpetvines, pink ceanothus, white abelia, and later, the clear lilac *Liriope muscari*. Autumn brings the mauve and violet of colchicum, and the bright yellow of the "fall daffodil," *Sternbergia lutea*. And winter is again ushered in with the spectacular red, pink, and white blossoms of *Camellia Sasanqua* and *C. oleifera*, together with the rare snowdrop *Galanthus corcyrensis*, which blooms in November and December and has set its seed by New Year's Day.

Camellia Sasanqua provides as showy a late fall and winter display as anyone could wish. It is reputed to be hardier than its more familiar relative, *C. japonica*, but the difference is actually in flowering time: all camellias are winter-flowering plants, native to areas where the seasons differ less than in this country. *C. Sasanqua*, which we think of as a fall-blooming plant, really has an earlier blooming season than *C. japonica*, which we think of as spring-blooming. Both species set flower buds in late summer. In the North, those of *C. japonica* must therefore endure longer periods of cold before they begin to open. The result is that the buds are sometimes winter-killed before they have a chance to show color, whereas those of *C. Sasanqua* start to bloom in fall and continue until truly cold weather sets in. For this reason, *Sasanqua* is probably the more satisfactory for northern

Flower Heads of Hydrangea

Pond at Sunset

gardens. All camellias, however, are really best suited to the South and to the West Coast. In the North they are difficult plants; even the comparatively mild winters of Delaware often take their toll, not only of buds, but of leaves and new growth.

Camellias, like azaleas, require an acid soil which is both well drained and moisture-retaining. They should be placed so that they receive as little winter sun and wind as possible. Camellias are members of the tea family, *Theaceae,* and are natives of Japan and China, the name *Camellia* commemorating a Moravian Jesuit missionary to the Orient, G.J. Kamel, who died in 1706. *Sasanqua* is the Japanese name for the species.

Each winter day at Winterthur is a small drama in itself. The sun rises over Clenny Run —a pale sun, but it warms the air. Sparrows, juncos, and bright cardinals begin calling in the shrubbery; perhaps later they will bathe in a stream. As the sun rises higher, the sound of running water seems to come from everywhere. Hundreds of tiny rivulets course beneath the rapidly disappearing snow, swelling the stream until it thunders, gorged and discolored, along its route toward the Brandywine. The snow retreats, leaving patches of sodden earth and dead grass, but also one of the brightest promises of spring—shoots of daffodils bristling along the banks of the stream like an army of green spears. But spring is not yet come. After the sun travels its brief journey across the sky and begins to sink, the cold returns. Birds go silently to roost. The gurgling water slows, and is stilled. The snow that remains freezes hard, and the puddles formed during the day become glazed with ice. All movement ceases as the sinking sun touches freezing ponds with purple and gold, and the air becomes thick with blue shadows and the silent cold of the winter night.

Clenny Run at Dawn

Spring at Winterthur is an endless medley of bird music: the organ notes of the wood thrush in the azalea woods; the bold whistle of the cardinal and the familiar caroling of the robin; the bell-like spring song of the blue jay, so different from his usual raucous cry; the throbbing of doves in the pines; the flute solo of song sparrows; and the trumpeting of the Canada geese who each spring rear their young on the Winterthur ponds. Bird music is a vital part of the beauty of Winterthur, from the first brittle song of the juncos among the melting winter snows to the moment when spring becomes summer, and bird song is replaced by the clamor of nestlings begging to be fed.

Spring

Spring at Winterthur is above all a season of color. The gaunt lines of winter are quickly veiled by unfolding leaves and opening flowers, and are finally obscured by bloom. Color moves in a series of waves through the season. The golf course in April is a sea of daffodils; in early May the Azalea Woods are bright with banks of pink, white, and red azaleas. Oak Hill in early May is a sheet of scarlet azalea 'Firefly,' and in late May it is white with deutzia and mock-orange. At every turn the eye is dazzled by a new expanse of color.

At the northeast edge of the Pinetum, near the very center of the garden, lies an area planted with shrubs that bloom as early in spring as weather permits. Visitors approach this area from the north, out of the Azalea Woods, and see it first as a distant haze of pale yellow and bright lavender beneath still leafless trees, a haze that proves to be dozens of yellow-flowered shrubs and azalea-like shrubs with large mauve blossoms. These are winter-hazels *(Corylopsis)* and Korean rhododendrons *(Rhododendron mucronulatum)*. The area is known, logically if not euphoniously, as the "Corylopsis-Mucronulatum Walk," and it is one of the first big displays of spring.

These plants begin to open their buds in early April, when trees are bare and winds still smell of winter. They reach their height of bloom the second or, if the spring is cool, the third week of the month. Although late frosts may injure the flowers, the unopened buds are seldom harmed, and usually replace the damaged blooms in a few days.

Winter-hazel belongs to the witch-hazel family, *Hamamelidaceae.* Of the dozen or so species in the genus—all native to the Orient and all bearing drooping clusters of pale yellow flowers in early spring—three are planted at Winterthur. Of these, *Corylopsis spicata,* the spiked winter-hazel, is by far the largest; it may become in time a small tree and most ungainly. The buttercup winter-hazel, *C. pauciflora,* although the most compact in growth, is unjustifiably called "dwarf." The least striking in bloom, it has sparser clusters of blossoms than other species. The broad-petaled winter-hazel, *C. platypetala,* is probably the most satisfactory of the three, for its flowers are as showy as those of *C. spicata,* and its habit of growth is as attractive as that of *C. pauciflora.* It is, however, difficult to obtain.

The most permanent of shrubs, winter-hazels are pleasing in habit, attractive in leaf, and seldom require pruning. They do best in humus-rich, somewhat acid soil, and, like

Daffodils and Sargent Cherry

Winter-Hazel.
Corylopsis

rhododendrons, thrive in the semi-shade of woodlands. Their only drawback for northern American gardens is their comparative lack of hardiness. Most species are fully hardy from New York south, but they are not recommended for areas north of western Pennsylvania, Kentucky, southern Kansas and Missouri.

The Korean rhododendron is one of the most satisfactory of the whole rhododendron family, for it is hardy throughout most of the United States, and it withstands droughty summer conditions peculiar to the eastern and central states much better than do most other rhododendrons. The plant grows to a height of six or eight feet, and is deciduous. Flat, two-inch flowers of bright mauve (pink in some forms) are produced in great abundance along naked branches in late March and early April. Its leaves are narrow and pointed *(mucro* means sharp point), about three inches long, and they turn to vivid bronze red or purple in the fall. Though commonly called "Korean azalea," it is not an azalea at all but a true rhododendron (the Korean azalea is properly *R. poukhanense)*.

Much confusion surrounds the terms azalea and rhododendron. Botanically, all azaleas are part of the genus *Rhododendron,* an immense aggregation of several hundred species divided by botanists into several subgroups called "series." *R. mucronulatum* and its close relative *R. dauricum* constitute the series *Dauricum.* The American *R. catawbiense* and *R. maximum,* ancestors of many of the large-leaved rhododendrons familiar in eastern gardens, belong to the series *Ponticum;* and plants such as *R. obtusum* (ancestor of the Kurume azaleas), *R. Schlippenbachi,* and *R. roseum* are members of the series *Azalea.* Though all azaleas

Winter-Hazel and Korean Rhododendron. *Corylopsis* and *R. mucronulatum*

Sargent Cherry at edge of Golf Course. *Prunus Sargenti*

may therefore be called rhododendrons, only those rhododendrons that belong to the series *Azalea* should be so called. Most members of this series are relatively important in gardens because they are of great ornamental value.

Gardening is a visual art, akin to painting in that it utilizes perspective and color to achieve its effect, and akin to sculpture in that it is three-dimensional. It differs from these arts, however, in that its medium consists of living, and therefore changing, elements. The gardener must be able not only to blend, accent, or restrain color, texture, line, and mass, but to see ahead, to determine whether a pleasing combination of colors in April will become a flat and lifeless monotony of green through the rest of spring and summer, or whether a planting of flowering trees and shrubs, which is architecturally attractive in summer and winter, will become unspeakably garish in flower.

The accompanying color photograph, taken in April, illustrates a finished composition which is in every way a success. The blossoms of flowering cherries, *Viburnum fragrans*, and *Rhododendron mucronulatum* cv. 'Cornell Pink' show soft pink and white against the blue green of white pines. In the background are other evergreens and the bare trunks and branches of oak, beech, and hickory. The specimen tree in the right foreground is a golden-rain tree, *Koelreuteria paniculata*. In April, its massive, dark branches provide just the right contrast to the flowers of the shrubs, emphasizing their brightness and delicacy.

In May and June, after the flowers fade, interest will be maintained by the fresh young foliage of the trees and shrubs, unfolding in many shades of green-tinted yellow, bronze, and red. In late June and July, the golden-rain tree, newly attired in bright green leaves, will put forth spikes of yellow flowers, followed by conspicuous green fruits in August.

Rhododendron mucronulatum cv. 'Cornell Pink' against "White Pines"

Heart-Leaved Bergenia.
B. cordifolia

Autumn will bring its own color and movement, when the leaves of the trees and shrubs begin to change color and fall to the ground. Winter will find the scene subdued in color, rather grim, but architecturally pleasing, with its contrasts of heavy and fine lines in the deciduous trees and shrubs, the infinite variations of ice and snow, and finally the promise of bright color as the buds of the rhododendrons begin to swell in late March.

Various ground cover plants, such as dogtooth-violets *(Erythronium Dens-canis)*, *E. revolutum*, and *E. tuolumnense*, hellebores, and the soft mauve-pink *Corydalis bulbosa*, supplement the corylopsis and Korean rhododendrons at Winterthur. Among the handsomest of these ground cover plants is *Bergenia cordifolia*, with its small, five-petaled flowers of rich rose borne on foot-high scapes ending in clusters that curl in gentle arabesques, and its rosettes of large, round, leathery leaves.

Bergenias do best in a rich soil that contains plenty of humus. They do not care for dry soils, but will thrive in either full sun or shade, and look especially well among woodland shrubs or in rock gardens. Unlike most plants called "herbaceous" (in contrast to woody shrubs), bergenias do not die down in winter, but are fully evergreen, which gives them added value in the garden.

Bergenia contains about half a dozen species, all native to eastern Asia. *Bergenia cordifolia*, hailing from Siberia and the hardiest and probably the most desirable species for American gardens, can be grown in most of the United States. Bergenias belong to the saxifrage family, *Saxifragaceae*. The genus commemorates the German botanist, Karl von Bergen.

'Cornell Pink' and Swiss Stone Pine. *Pinus cembra*

Christmas-Rose.
Helleborus niger

Certain color motifs run through the seasons at Winterthur like bright threads through a tapestry. Again and again, the combination of yellow and lavender or mauve appears—in the golden adonis and lavender *Crocus Tomasinianus* in late winter, in the pale yellow *Rhododendron Keiskei* and the mauve *R. poukhanense* in late April, and, also in late April, in the yellow of the golden currant *(Ribes aureum)* and the warm mauve of *carolinianum* hybrid rhododendrons. But this motif nowhere appears in such splendor as in the combination of *Corylopsis* and *Rhododendron mucronulatum*. These two colors, so expressive of spring, are perfectly complementary.

Combining colors, whether in a painting, a room, or a garden, is a highly complex art. There are infinite variations of colors, and disaster stalks the unwary gardener who masses them without taking heed of their overtones. The yellow of corylopsis, for example, is a pale but pure color, with very little green or orange in it—a "cool" yellow. The mauve of the Korean rhododendron is in contrast a warm color, containing pink and red. If one were to combine Korean rhododendron and the common forsythia, the result would very likely be unpleasant, for the yellow of the common forsythia is one of the hottest, most intense colors imaginable. The yellow of most daffodils is also hot, so the only daffodil growing in the corylopsis-mucronulatum planting is a cultivar, 'Hunter's Moon,' which was chosen for its pale lemon color. Like all successful art, this color combination is deceptively simple.

Early-blooming plants depend much more on weather conditions than do those of late

Corsican Hellebore. *Helleborus corsicus*

The Hellebore Walk

spring and summer. At Winterthur, one can safely predict that the first day of June will see the deutzias and mock-oranges in bloom, but one cannot be certain of seeing snowdrops on the first day of February. If the winter has been mild, snowdrops may appear in January; if it has been severe, they may not appear until March. So it is with the fabled Christmas-rose or black hellebore, *Helleborus niger;* in mild England, it may appear at Christmas or even before, but here it seldom begins to bloom until after the first true thaw, in January, February, or as late as March.

The Christmas-rose grows along a path leading through the planting of corylopsis and *R. mucronulatum* called the "Hellebore Walk." Here also, together with such low-growing plants as bergenias, dogtooth-violets, and mauve corydalis, all of which harmonize with the corylopsis and rhododendrons, are other species of hellebore, including several varieties of the Lenten-rose, *Helleborus orientalis*, and Corsican hellebore, *H. corsicus* (also known as *H. lividus*). All hellebores are herbaceous perennials with evergreen or half-evergreen leaves and large waxy flowers of various shades: white in *H. niger*, apple green in *H. corsicus*, and whitish, pinkish, purplish, or green in *H. orientalis*. All bloom very early in the spring— the earliest, *H. niger*, begins to bloom in late winter—and all are attractive when out of flower because of their handsome, deep green, divided foliage, which in *H. corsicus* resembles holly. They are native to Europe and western Asia, and in nature are plants of woodlands and shaded hillsides.

Hellebores grow best in deep, rich soil, enriched with leaf mold and rotted manure. Since winter winds may injure their attractive evergreen foliage, a shaded site is preferable, and a light mulch of evergreen branches helps during the winter. It is important, however,

Daffodils on Clenny Run

not to mulch the plants too heavily, because they are prone to rot if they cannot get sufficient light and air during winter warm spells. Hellebores are closely related to peonies, and like peonies they resent disturbance and are slow to reestablish after transplanting. Like peonies, also, they prefer a slightly sweet soil, so that an application of ground limestone every few years is beneficial in the acid-soil regions of the East. Hellebores are hardy in the more temperate areas of this country, but are not recommended for northern New England, the North Central states, or the Western Mountain states because of susceptibility to winter-kill in extreme cold.

Spring so abounds in color that the eye sometimes misses subtle details of form and texture. For example, the gaunt bole of white pine contrasts with the frothy blossoms of Korean rhododendron, and the rugged bark of flowering cherry contrasts with both its own delicate flowers and the soft carpet of daffodils beneath it. Contrasts like these give strength and body to a garden scene: the balance of opposing forces, dark and light, bright and dull, massive and delicate.

Daffodils and Sargent Cherry

Occasionally, however, the simple massing of blooms suits perfectly the purpose of the gardener. Near the corylopsis-mucronulatum planting lies a golf course, which, with its thousands of naturalized daffodils, provides a wonderful combination of the functional and the beautiful. In April the rough along each fairway comes alive with masses of gold and white, making this expanse of grass, viewed from a distance, a sheet of color. Accenting the massed daffodils are trees such as the magnificent red oak, and flowering trees such as the two ancient Sargent cherries.

People often ask what the difference is between a daffodil and a narcissus. Actually, the terms are roughly interchangeable, since daffodil is the common name for most members of the genus *Narcissus*. Gardeners tend to use "daffodil" for varieties of the trumpet section, and "narcissus" for the short-cupped varieties such as the pheasant's-eye or poet's narcissus, but since trumpet and cupped varieties have been extensively intercrossed in recent years, the distinction is sometimes hard to make. One of course cannot go wrong if he calls them all narcissi. "Jonquil" is a third term that adds to the confusion, but this name is best reserved for narcissi of the section *Jonquilla,* all of which have narrow, rush-like leaves and several small short-cupped flowers per stem. True jonquils are not at all common in American gardens.

There is more variation in form, color, and season of bloom in the genus *Narcissus* than most people realize. At Winterthur the tiny *Narcissus minimus (N. asturiensis)*, a perfect golden trumpet daffodil in miniature which seldom exceeds three inches in height, blooms with squills and crocuses in late March. It is quickly followed by *N. minor,* a slightly larger golden trumpet, by *N. nanus,* a still larger golden trumpet, and finally, in early April, by

Korean Rhododendron and White Pine at edge of Azalea Woods

The Sycamore and Narcissi

the full-sized golden trumpet *N. Pseudo-narcissus*, the common, old-fashioned but still lovely daffodil celebrated by Wordsworth which ushers in the daffodil season. Scattered throughout the gardens, the product of many years of constant planting, thousands upon thousands of daffodils begin to open.

Not all garden varieties of daffodils can thrive under the rather rugged, semi-wild conditions that naturalized bulbs must endure. Among those that have been consistently successful at Winterthur are: 'Emperor,' a medium yellow trumpet, the white trumpet 'Beersheba,' the large-cupped cream and orange 'Dick Wellband' and 'Franciscus Drake,' the rich yellow jonquil hybrid 'Trevithian,' the red and white short-cupped 'Firetail,' the double 'Twink,' and, of course, the lovely white, red-eyed poet's narcissus or pheasant's-eye, *Narcissus poeticus*, which blooms later and prefers somewhat damp conditions (as along the banks of streams or ponds). Generally speaking, the short-cupped varieties begin blooming somewhat later than the trumpets, and the pheasant's-eye blooms later still, beginning to show in early May. Latest of all narcissi at Winterthur is a small species of jonquil, the rush-leaved jonquil, *N. juncifolius*, which bears its butter yellow flowers in late May along with deutzias, camassias, and azalea 'Magnifica.'

Visitors to Winterthur will notice two things about the daffodils: mixing of varieties is rigorously avoided, and the beds or drifts are extremely irregular in shape. Nothing gives so patchy an effect as a large mixed planting of daffodils—some tall, some short; some yellow, some white, and some bicolored; some going to seed as others begin to open. Uniformity is the great virtue here. A drift of yellow trumpets may contrast beautifully with a drift of white nearby, but mixing within the beds themselves is disastrous. Uniformity

The Lookout and Daffodils

Daffodils
on Clenny Run

can of course become the vice of monotony. To counteract this, the daffodils at Winterthur are planted by means of an interesting and, so far as I know, unique method developed years ago by Mr. du Pont. Once the dimensions of a new bed have been roughly determined, fallen branches are used to outline it. The result is a series of gracefully irregular curves—the pleasing lines of nature itself.

Much of the charm of spring bulbs such as daffodils lies in their evanescence. They begin to bloom almost as soon as they emerge from the bare ground, and they disappear completely before the advent of summer; thus they seem as brief and fleeting as spring itself. In this they differ from the flowering trees and shrubs of spring which change with the seasons but are always before us.

Another early spring flower is the pasqueflower, *Anemone Pulsatilla*. Its common name, "Easter flower" in Old French, comes originally from the Hebrew word for Passover, and refers to the plant's blooming in April, near the time of both Easter and Passover. Beautiful indeed are the rich, mauve-blue flowers, and almost as beautiful are the plumed seed heads which follow them. The pasqueflower, a member of the buttercup family, *Ranunculaceae*, is native to Europe. It is easily cultivated in the United States, yet it is not often seen in gardens. Rich or poor soils suit it well, as long as they are well drained.

The Winterthur Museum rests on a gentle, south-facing slope in the rolling hills of northern Delaware. The soil of these hills is nearly neutral, and contains very little humus, yet, because of years of dedicated attention and good gardening techniques, plants of all

Daffodils on Golf Course

Saucer Magnolia and Museum. *M.* × *Soulangiana*

kinds flourish at Winterthur. Great expanses of lawn, broken only by occasional flowering trees and shrubs and the immense oaks, beeches, and tulip-trees that are the remnant of original forests, surround the Museum. Up the slope to the north stands one of the most spectacular of flowering trees, a tall, white, ancient *Magnolia* × *Soulangiana* almost as old as Winterthur itself.

Magnolia × *Soulangiana* is one of the most widely used flowering trees in America. It has become almost a status symbol in suburban gardens which is unfortunate, for in its common pink-purple forms it is so imposing and dominating a tree that it demands great space around it. The white forms are only a little less spectacular. *Magnolia* × *Soulangiana* is a hybrid of the exquisite white *M. denudata* and the purple *M. liliflora*. From the former it inherits size and a measure of the beauty of that species; from the latter it inherits purple coloration and its habit of blooming when very small, which in part explains its popularity. In the large landscape of Winterthur there is room for even these overwhelming plants. Other magnolias in the garden include plants of a pink clone called 'San Jose,' other clones in the pinkish range, and a very old planting of various pinks and the deep pink-purple 'Lennei.'

"Saucer magnolia" is the correct common name for *M.* × *Soulangiana*. It is often mis-called "tulip tree," a pleasingly descriptive name, but one which causes confusion with the true tulip-tree or tulip-poplar, *Liriodendron tulipifera*. The usual blooming season is late April and early May, when the huge flowers are borne in abundance on leafless branches. In some varieties a scattering of blooms appears during the summer months. The most consistent summer bloomer is the purplish 'Lennei.'

Magnolia × *Soulangiana* is hardy throughout most of the United States. It is one of the easiest magnolias to grow, but, like the rest of the genus, demands a fairly rich, slightly acid soil, with plenty of moisture during the growing season. All magnolias are somewhat

Pasqueflower. *Anemone Pulsatilla*

East Terrace of Museum

difficult to transplant because their fleshy roots rot quickly if cut or injured. For this reason it is better to get small specimens and plant them in spring instead of autumn so that damaged roots will break into growth quickly and thus reestablish the plant. The genus *Magnolia* honors Pierre Magnol (1638–1715), French botanist and director of the famous gardens at Montpellier.

East of the Museum, a wide terrace overlooks a wooded area and swimming pool which, like the golf course, combines utility with floral beauty. Just below the pool is a small summer garden of foxgloves, anthemis, thalictrum, daylilies, and various annuals. Around the pool deep blue lobelias, pink begonias, and pink *Sedum Sieboldii* are arranged in large pots. Ivy and variegated *Vinca major* cascade from decorated lead tanks. Shrubs such as azaleas, lavenders, and tree peonies grow in raised beds near the walks. Even the diving board has a *Euonymus Fortunei vegetus* clambering over its base. A great flight of stairs between banks of azaleas leads down from the east terrace to the wrought iron gate of the swimming pool.

On a nearby wall grow English ivy *(Hedera helix)* and Colchis ivy *(Hedera colchica)*. The Colchis ivy is an extremely attractive vine which could serve many purposes in our gardens, yet is almost unknown in America. Its great, burnished leaves are much larger than those of the common English ivy; under good growing conditions they reach ten inches in length. It makes a striking cover for walls, and is perhaps even more effective as a ground cover. Although it lacks hardiness, in Delaware it is completely hardy, and should be suitable wherever temperatures stay above zero for most of the winter. When bruised, the leaves of this plant smell exactly like celery, which makes it easily identifiable.

View from East Terrace

Hedera colchica is native to Asia Minor and the Caucasus—the Colchis of the ancient Greeks.

A visitor to Winterthur will notice more than masses of color or individual plants. He will note occasional openings along the wooded paths that draw his gaze into the distance: to a quiet pond, a summerhouse at the top of a hill, the gold of forsythia or the crimson of azaleas along the edge of a wood. None of these views is accidental. Each has been designed to lead the eye momentarily from the immediate to the far-off, for nothing becomes more wearisome than acre on acre of densely planted gardens. The eye longs to leap away from a deluge of color; vistas provide the opportunity. A good vista should be soothing enough to induce the visitor to rest for a moment, yet interesting enough to entice him onward.

One of the most successful vistas at Winterthur is the view down the long stairs from the east terrace of the Museum to the swimming pool. Billowing masses of box and pink azaleas form a frame which leads the eye down the line of the stairs to the rectangular pool below. Halfway down the steps is a landing which momentarily interrupts the vista, for a path leads off to the left through a woodland carpeted with countless squills and

Pink Fawn-Lily.
Erythronium revolutum

chionodoxas. In late March and early April the whole floor of the wood shimmers with a blue haze of flowers. The path leads past two spring-fed pools filled with great, slow, golden carp, and ends finally at the March Walk.

Near the end of this path, and on the March Walk itself, grows a profusion of lovely little bulbous plants variously called trout-lilies, fawn-lilies, adder's-tongues, and dogtooth-violets. The several species here include the native *Erythronium americanum,* its yellow flowers and deep green leaves speckled with red like the sides of a trout. Perhaps the most beautiful of all is a species from the Far West, *E. revolutum,* which in April carries its deep pink lily-flowers on gracefully recurved scapes above leaves of glossy green and maroon. Erythroniums have a rather peculiar distribution. One species is native to Europe and two to the eastern half of the United States; many others are confined to the Western Mountain states and the Pacific Coast. These western erythroniums are by far the showiest and most desirable species in the genus, but unfortunately they are not easy to grow in eastern gardens. Dryness especially affects them adversely, and at Winterthur they grow best in damp, partially shaded positions. In fact, a colony of *E. revolutum* on the upper end of the March Walk flourishes in a bank which is wet from the seepage of springs most of the year. Standing moisture would probably rot them, but water bubbling through the ground around them, as it does in their mountain home, seems to suit them perfectly.

The March Walk by no means ceases to be interesting in March, for there is a succession of bloom here from the moment the winter snows melt until late summer. When the very

Torch Azaleas and Ostrich Ferns. *Rhododendron Kaempferi* and *Pteretis nodulosa*

earliest bulb flowers fade, other bulbs and wildflowers—violets, anemones, bellworts, and Virginia bluebells—replace them. In May, torch azaleas bloom in the glade east of the March Walk, their salmony red flowers contrasting beautifully with the apple green of young fern fronds. In June, in the same glade, *Rhododendron maximum* opens white flowers from pink buds; later the orange of the tawny daylily *(Hemerocallis fulva),* and the purple blue of the wandering bellflower *(Campanula rapunculoides)* and the old-fashioned "August-lily" *(Hosta ventricosa)* brighten the green shade of the summer trees.

Of the fifteen or so species of *Erythronium* native to America, the large-flowered fawn-lily, *E. grandiflorum,* is unsurpassed for size and sheer showiness. "Large-flowered" is simply a translation of the Latin *grandiflorum;* more pleasing is the name by which it is known in its native haunts, "glacier-lily." The glacier-lily inhabits mountain slopes from British Columbia south to Oregon and east to Idaho. Its nodding flowers of sun yellow are borne singly or in pairs on foot-high scapes, and each of the six segments is strongly recurved, so that the flowers look like miniature Turk's-cap lilies. But the leaves are different from those of most fawn-lilies in being unmottled and glossy. At Winterthur the glacier-lily grows on a grassy, semi-shaded bank above the March Walk, where it blooms in April.

Glacier-Lily.
Erythronium grandiflorum

Fairly dependable in cultivation, it does not thrive in dry soils, although it requires less moisture than *E. revolutum*. American erythroniums have a reputation for difficulty which is in part justified, for they are certainly more difficult to grow than, say, daffodils. Still, with proper precautions they can be grown well, and their beauty warrants a little extra care. Adequate moisture is their first prerequisite. The second is a good, woodsy, humus-rich soil. The third is deep planting, as anyone knows who has attempted to transplant the eastern trout-lily from the woods and has come away with six inches of white underground stem and no bulb at all. When an erythronium seed germinates on the forest floor, it produces a single leaf and a small solid bulb; during the second year, the bulb puts out one or more long, threadlike runners called "droppers" which burrow down through the soil at an angle of about forty degrees, each producing a new bulb. This process is repeated every year until the new bulbs reach a depth of several inches. Finally, the plants, now many instead of one, begin to flower, and no more droppers are formed. When erythronium bulbs, especially immature bulbs, are planted too shallowly in the garden, they are apt to revert to producing droppers; deep planting guards against this. Various species differ in their propensity to put out droppers—moisture and friability of soil also play a part in the process—but a good rule of thumb is to plant all erythroniums at least four inches deep.

The genus is closely related to both tulips and true lilies, and belongs of course to the lily family, *Liliaceae*. The scientific name is derived from the Greek *erythros*, "red," and

Greek Windflower.
Anemone blanda

alludes to the red-purple markings on the flowers of the one European species. Much more fanciful are the various common names of these plants: "adder's-tongue" is an allusion to the forked, pointed appearance of the leaves as they emerge from the ground; "dog-tooth-violet" refers to the shape of the white bulbs of some species, which are long and curved like a canine tooth; "fawn-lily" and "trout-lily" refer to the dappled, mottled, or speckled leaves of many of the species.

Anemone is a large and varied genus with representatives in Europe, Asia, and America. Some grow from tubers and others from fibrous roots; some bloom early in the spring and others in fall; several are beautiful. One of the earliest is the Greek windflower, *Anemone blanda*, which opens its deep violet-blue, yellow-centered flowers at Winterthur in early April. The flowers of these tiny plants are daisy-like in appearance, though not in structure. Their form and color are reminiscent of the hardy asters or Michaelmas daisies that brighten American fields and roadsides in autumn, although they are not even remotely related to daisies or asters. Along with peonies, hellebores, columbines, aconites, larkspurs, and bugbanes, they are members of the ancient and botanically primitive family of buttercups.

Many anemones grow wild in the Near East, and references to them are nearly as old as recorded history. The biblical "lilies of the field" that outshone even the splendor of Solomon were probably the scarlet and black *A. pavonina*. No lilies grow wild in the fields of Israel, but the landscape blazes with anemones during the spring of the year. The name itself is thought to be drived directly from the Greek *anemos,* wind, but it most likely comes ultimately from the Syrian *nama'an,* the cry of lament uttered when the god of spring, Tammuz, suffered his annual death in the autumn. Tammuz, like his Greek counterpart Adonis, shed his blood on the earth, and scarlet anemones sprang into bloom.

Anemone blanda is more modest than its brilliant relatives from the Holy Land, but it is also much more amenable to cultivation in this country. Its blackish twisted tubers should be planted in early fall, two or three inches deep, in sun or shade. It is quite tolerant of poor soil, but it responds to generous additions of humus in the form of peat or leaf mold. Fortunately, most bulb dealers stock it, and it is so inexpensive that large numbers can be purchased at a reasonable price. Lovely as the individual flowers are, they seem even more beautiful in company with dozens of their fellows.

If only one word could describe the Winterthur gardens, it would probably be "informal." Of the sixty-odd acres of gardens, only the Sundial Garden and the Museum terraces could by any stretch of the imagination be called formal. The rest is a combination of the natural and artificial, so well blended that the changes seem made not by man but by nature herself. The secret of this art that conceals art is a skillful conservation and manipulation of native plants. At Winterthur, native plants are rarely replaced by exotic ones. Instead, exotics are used in combination with native plants, which may be thinned or pruned to accommodate them but are seldom exterminated. Still less often are existing trees cut away. A garden without trees is a dull place, and a fully mature tree cannot be purchased at any price.

One of the most naturalistic areas of Winterthur is the Quarry. Great outcroppings of rock, in whose crevices grow ferns, mosses, and flowering plants, project from the sheer walls of a deep basin through which several spring-fed streams meander. On the cool, wet floor of this basin grow masses of primulas—soft lavender and white *Primula denticulata* in early spring, and tall candelabra primulas in many colors in late spring and early summer. Many native plants grow in the wet areas also, and thrive with the primulas among rocks that line the little stream flowing from the Quarry down to Clenny Run. In the April view shown here, the Quarry bridge is in the far background, and the Bristol Summerhouse tops the rise to the right. In the foreground are masses of white *Arabis procurrens,* a rock cress from southern Europe.

In early April, a visitor on the bridge sees the colorful view illustrated here. The yellow cups of the marsh-marigold, *Caltha palustris,* glisten in the shallow water beneath the bridge. These plants of one of our earliest blooming native perennials were dug from woodland bogs on other parts of the estate. Beyond the marsh-marigolds is an expanse of one of the most delightful plants in nature, *Primula denticulata,* which late in March begins to show, at ground level, mauve or white flowers in globular heads the size of tennis balls. As the season advances, these balls rise up on stout stems ultimately a foot in height, and the flowers stay in good condition through much of April. *P. denticulata,* a native of the Himalayas, is one of the most dependable of the Asiatic primulas.

Tall oaks and beeches, majestic on their cliffside perch, rise around the rim of the Quarry. On the east side they shade a pleasant retreat for visitors—a stone terrace where one may sit and observe. There is always something to see in the Quarry: on the bank that rises to the Bristol Summerhouse, dwarf bearded irises, late-blooming satsuki azaleas, dwarf forsythias, autumn snowflakes, hardy cyclamen, and many other interesting plants bloom pleasingly at eye level.

To walk down the wide, irregular stone steps into the Quarry is to enter a different world. The air is cooler and moister than the air above, as if charged with the vapor of mountain cataracts and chilled by melting snows. Water gurgles from the springs all summer long. Robins and catbirds splash in the puddles. Water thrushes teeter like mechanical

Marsh-Marigolds and Himalayan Primula in Quarry. *Caltha palustris* and *P. denticulata*

Mountain-Andromeda.
Pieris floribunda

toys along the dripping ledges of rock. Occasionally a scarlet tanager descends from the treetops in a flash of glowing red and velvety black.

The Quarry is a kind of microcosm, cut off, distinct from the rest of the gardens. Moss-hung, fern-covered rocks are reminiscent of Vermont mountains; Japan is represented by the brown-felted, ribbon-like foliage of *Rhododendron Makinoi*, the sweet white spires of *Clethra barbinervis*, and the bold, quilted leaves of *Hosta Sieboldiana;* here too are primulas from high Himalayan bogs, bearberry from New Jersey pine barrens, marsh-marigold and swamp-pink from Delaware swamps. Even the names of the plants have a special glamour: *Andromeda, Zenobia, Pieris, Leucothoe*. A list of the Quarry plants reads like a roster of Greek mythology.

A bit of Appalachia appears with *Pieris floribunda,* the mountain-andromeda. This is an excellent evergreen shrub, lower growing and hardier than its much more common relative, the Japanese *P. japonica*. Its spikes of white, urn-shaped flowers in April are quite handsome, but the plant is more valuable for its burnished, evergreen foliage. Since it seldom exceeds four feet in height, it is ideal for large rockeries, and also makes a good woodland or border shrub. It thrives under the same conditions as do its relatives, rhododendrons and azaleas. A member of the heath family, *Ericaceae,* it is hardy in all but the coldest New England and North Central states.

Many alpine and rock plants grow with the mountain-andromeda in the Quarry. Blooming in April are the dwarf, orange, native columbine, *Aquilegia canadensis;* the delicate

Judas Tree overlooking Quarry. *Cercis canadensis*

Barrenwort. *Epimedium*

white *Viola blanda;* bluets or quaker-ladies, *Houstonia caerulea,* like hundreds of blue-white stars; wintergreen or teaberry, *Gaultheria procumbens;* and yellow star-grass, *Hypoxis hirsuta.* These are all natives. An unusual rock plant from China flourishes with them in great abundance: *Corydalis cheilanthifolia,* the fern-leaved corydalis. This plant, closely related to bleeding-hearts and Dutchman's-breeches, is extremely rare in cultivation. It does not do well under ordinary garden conditions, and in fact seems to require the free drainage and lack of competition from other plants that rockeries provide. But it thrives in the Quarry.

Corydalis has an interesting history at Winterthur. The specimens of this plant in the Quarry are descendants of a few purchased in the early 1930's as landscaping material for the rocky banks below the east terrace of the Museum. Ordinarily somewhat difficult to establish, these plants for some reason quickly took hold and seeded themselves in the rocks near the fish pools. Over the years the area was allowed to grow up with wild plants, but the corydalis thrived untended for nearly three decades, and was happily at hand when the Quarry was developed in 1961.

Nature has endowed most rock plants with an unequaled delicacy and grace, as though compensating for the harshness of the situations in which they grow. The leaves of *Corydalis cheilanthifolia* are as graceful as those of any fern, and the sulphur yellow flowers borne on spikes in early spring offer an airy contrast to the rough rocks. Other graceful rock plants are the barrenworts *(Epimedium),* which are as valuable for their handsome foliage as for their flowers. Of the species in the Quarry, one of the most handsome is *E. alpinum rubrum,* with deep pink flowers. Others are the white *E. grandiflorum niveum* and the yellow *E. pinnatum.* Native to much of the north temperate zone, epimediums bloom early in spring and are quite hardy. Unlike most rock plants, they are easy to grow in borders if the soil is rich, moist, and well drained, and if they have some protection from the sun during the hottest part of the day. Since they seldom exceed a foot in height, they also

Fern-Leaved Corydalis. *C. cheilanthifolia*

Cinnamon Fern.
Osmunda cinnamomea

make excellent ground cover. They are herbaceous perennials, belonging to the barberry family, *Berberidaceae*.

Ferns have been planted freely in the Quarry. Among the rocks are the tall evergreen Christmas fern and marginal woodfern, the tiny polypody, the graceful spleenworts, and the minute, mat-forming *Woodsia ilvensis*. In the moister soil on the floor of the Quarry grow the taller species, such as the interrupted, the royal, the ostrich, and the cinnamon ferns. The cinnamon fern *(Osmunda cinnamomea)*, as it springs in April or early May from the black mold of the Quarry, is as typical of spring as the brightest flower. Pale green in color, and covered by a rufous down, each shoot or "fiddlehead," is actually a tightly rolled leaf, or frond, of the fern. In their juvenile state, these fronds are much esteemed as a cooked vegetable by connoisseurs of exotic foods, being reputedly as tasty as the finest asparagus.

The cinnamon fern is native to both North America and Eurasia, and is abundant in swamps and wet woodlands in Delaware. It grows occasionally to a height of six feet, and thrives in shade or, provided the soil is naturally somewhat damp, in sun. *Osmunda* is a latinization of *Osmunder*, the Old English name for the god Thor. *Cinnamomea* refers to the cinnamon colored down which covers the young fronds (especially the young fruiting fronds) but which disappears as the plant ages.

Thus, with its ferns and flowering plants, tall trees and year-round murmur of running water, the Quarry is always a beautiful spot. In April, when wildflowers bloom in the

Pond Below Quarry

rocks and early primulas on the floor, thousands of blue squills and chionodoxas carpet the woodland above the rim. These are soon followed by masses of old-fashioned yellow daffodils, *Narcissus Pseudo-narcissus*, whose wild grace lends itself to woodland planting, and by *Phlox divaricata, P. stolonifera*, and *Mertensia virginica*—all in soft shades of blue. In April also, on the bank east of the Quarry, several old redbud or Judas trees *(Cercis canadensis)* burst into bloom above a bed of the dwarf pale yellow *Forsythia viridissima bronxensis*.

Water is invaluable in gardens. It attracts birds of all sorts and gives the illusion of coolness on hot days. If it is running it is pleasant to hear, and if it is still it is pleasant to see, for it then becomes a kind of mirror of nature. Flowing through the center of Winterthur in its course towards the Brandywine, Clenny Run fills several ponds. Water from these ponds irrigates the whole garden during summer droughts, and has saved many priceless plants. In addition, the ponds bring an extra bounty of beauty all the year round. Herons haunt their shores in summer, and the rattling cry of kingfishers sounds throughout most of the year. Mallard ducks and Canada geese feed and nest on them, and rare fowl, such as wandering gulls or fish hawks, or wild ducks such as teal, widgeon, or ring-necks often appear during their migration. Swifts and swallows use them on summer afternoons for their baths on the wing, and regularly each autumn a solitary loon visits one of them on his way south, making the evenings ring with his unearthly wail.

Illustrated here are two aspects of a small pond below the Quarry. On a quiet day in April, the tall trees, the rocks, and the white *Arabis procurrens* are reflected on its still surface, producing a scene in which the details of reality are slightly blurred, even distorted, as in an Impressionist painting. Here, on such a day, the tranquility of the scene may be disturbed by the appearance of the "Winterthur geese" and their annual brood. The same pond is the focal point of a long eastern vista from the top of Oak Hill, a vista which approaches perfection in early May when the hillside blazes with the scarlet azalea 'Firefly,' and the meadow below is aflame with *Primula japonica*.

The skies above the Sundial Garden are higher and bluer in spring than at any other time of the year; the clouds are softer and whiter. And on the ground are all the lovely colors of spring: cloud white of magnolia, blush pink of cherry and flowering almond, mauve of lilac, and sky blue of wild phlox. The air is heavy with the sweetness of lilacs, the musk of viburnums, the sharp perfume of magnolias. One wanders from plant to plant, intoxicated by form and color and fragrance—by spring itself. And when one finally, reluctantly, leaves and looks back, he finds the grassy, plant-lined corridors down which he just walked resolved into a mass of pink, mauve, and white, so delicate that it seems to shimmer like a mirage against the dark, solid presence of the Pinetum behind it.

The star magnolias are the vanguard of the Sundial Garden. Winter is hardly over when their buds shed downy gray coats and swell into pinkish white blossoms. This is the very first magnolia to flower at Winterthur, beginning so early in April that the blooms are often browned by frost. *Magnolia stellata* grows into a small, spreading tree fifteen or, at most, twenty feet in height, with leaves three to four inches in length, and flowers—sometimes pink but more often pure white—three inches across. The flowers are composed of many narrow segments, their total effect being delicate and starry, hence both the common and the scientific names *(stellata* is Latin for "starry"). Less common in American gardens than the more spectacular saucer magnolia *(Magnolia × Soulangiana),* the star magnolia is a better plant for the small garden. Blooming when quite small, it is one of the most attractive magnolias in winter. Also, it is much less overpowering, and it possesses a grace and delicacy that the saucer magnolia lacks.

The rectangle enclosed by box hedge which today is called the Sundial Garden was once a recreation area. One level, where the sundial now stands, was a tennis court, and a lower level, now planted with lilacs and flowering cherries, was a croquet court. In

Azaleas on Oak Hill. *Rhododendron* cv. 'Firefly'

Star Magnolia.
M. stellata

1957 the courts were made into gardens, though not without certain difficulties; paving and years of use had combined with naturally stony soil to produce an element so water-resistant that the new garden became a lake after every rain. This condition was finally remedied by dynamiting deep fissures in the underlying rock.

The center of this garden today is the sundial, around which are arranged in a circular pattern four curved beds of the dwarf evergreen privet honeysuckle *(Lonicera pileata)*. In a larger circle around these are four more curved beds, thickly planted with early white spireas, pink flowering almonds, and pink and salmon flowering quinces *(Chaenomeles)*. Two immense specimens of pink and white *Chaenomeles* cv. 'Appleblossom,' underplanted with lavender-blue *Phlox stolonifera* and *P. divaricata,* stand at opposite ends of the two beds to the north, and frame a view of the Chaenomeles Walk, a wide grass path which leads down from the Pinetum and is lined with colorful flowering quinces. At the foot of this walk, fragrant early viburnums, such as *V. Carlesii, V. bitchiuense, V.* × *Burkwoodi,* and *V.* × *Juddii,* perfume the air in late April.

Viburnum is a large genus of shrubs native to both hemispheres, nearly every member of which is extremely ornamental—the kinds of plants the great collector Ernest Henry Wilson discussed in his *Aristocrats of the Garden.* Some viburnums, such as *V. Carlesii* and its close allies, are grown primarily for their sweetly scented flowers. Others, including *V. setigerum* and *V. nudum,* are grown for their spectacular berries. Still others are grown for both showiness of bloom and of fruit. Almost all have good foliage and habit, and all have an

The Sundial Garden

air of quality about them, a kind of distinction that marks them as superior plants.

Blooming at the foot of the Chaenomeles Walk a short time after *V. Carlesii* and its cohorts is an extraordinary viburnum, *V. macrocephalum sterile*, the "Chinese snowball." With its gray branches and trunk, and its gray-green, persistent leaves, this large shrub is attractive the year round, but in May it becomes a spectacle when huge clusters of white flowers, sometimes nearly a foot across, cover the plant. It is perhaps too emphatically showy for the very small garden, but in surroundings which harmonize with its own grand lines it comes into its own. Not the least of its virtues is a long blooming season. The whole flower cluster emerges in miniature from a rough wooly bud early in the spring, and grows slowly, passing from bright green to creamy white at maturity in May. When the Chaenomeles Walk and the Sundial Garden are attired in pink, mauve, salmon, and white in late April, the nearly mature flower heads of the Chinese snowball, now an intense chartreuse, make an unexpected and extremely effective transition between the conventional spring colors and the solemn, deep green of the conifers in the Pinetum.

The flowers of *Viburnum macrocephalum sterile*, like the flowers of all "snowballs," lack

Chinese Snowball. *Viburnum macrocephalum sterile*

generative parts. Many viburnums have clusters of flowers which consist of a center of small, unshowy, fertile flowers surrounded by a ring of large, showy, sterile flowers. Snow-balls are simply mutations in which the clusters consist entirely of sterile flowers. Such mutations eventually die out in the wild since they lack the capacity to reproduce them-selves, but they live on in gardens by man's desire. The role of fertile flowers is to re-produce the species; therefore they wither and go to seed as soon as they are pollinated by insects. Sterile flowers of course cannot go to seed. They remain unpollinated, usually lasting much longer than fertile flowers.

Of the three snowballs in cultivation, the hardiest and most common in American gardens from Zone 3 southward is the European snowball, *V. opulus roseum*. Unfortunately, this is the least desirable, because it is susceptible to infestation by aphids which mars its appearance. Less common and slightly less hardy in Zone 3 is the Japanese snowball, *V. tomentosum plicatum*, a much more desirable garden plant. Neither is as spectacular as the Chinese snowball, but both are hardier, the Japanese plant being probably the better choice for temperate climates. The Chinese snowball is reputed to be unreliably hardy north of Washington, D.C. Those at Winterthur, however, have thrived, undisturbed by winter frosts, for well over fifty years. It should certainly be the first choice among snowballs in areas where winter temperatures seldom fall below zero. Viburnums belong to the honey-suckle family, *Caprifoliaceae*.

During the last week of April, the southwest corner of the Pinetum is alight with the

royal azalea *(Rhododendron Schlippenbachi)*, the air shimmering with the pinkness of sun passing through the almost translucent blossoms. In these flowers, perched like huge, pale pink butterflies on leafless stems, or littering the ground beneath each bush, we see the passage of time more clearly than in the hands of a clock or on the pages of a calendar. We see mortality firsthand. But we also see something of the wholeness of nature's cycle. Life is change, and a garden would indeed be a dead spot if it did not alter according to season. One reason the artificial flowers so popular today will never take the place of the real thing is precisely that they do not die; they last too long, collecting dust forever. Regardless of how perfectly they resemble real flowers, one always feels that they are somehow more dead than the most withered flower in the garden. They do not change; therefore they never live.

The royal azalea is one of the most ornamental members of a notably ornamental family. Its three-inch flowers, borne in great abundance on naked branches in late April and early May, are pale pink to white in some forms, and quite unusual in shape: the lateral lobes of the corolla are elongated so that the flower is distinctly butterfly-shaped. Its leaves, unusual for an azalea, are three to five inches long, broadly spoon-shaped, and clustered in whorls at the tips of the branches. The plant is completely deciduous, and not the least of its attractions is the pale green of its foliage in summer and the fine orange color in fall. The habit of the shrub is broad and spreading when grown in full sun, and its ultimate height is about six feet. It does best (in Delaware, at least) in full sun or very light shade, and seems to withstand dry conditions and non-acid soil better than most azaleas. Native to northeastern China, Korea, and northern Japan, it is one of the hardiest of the genus. At the Arnold Arboretum in Boston, where in 1905 it was first introduced in America, it is completely hardy, and has proved satisfactory throughout most of New England. The plants at Winterthur (which undoubtedly came from the Arnold Arboretum shortly after 1905) have never been affected by winter cold.

R.Schlippenbachi is a true azalea, the best known representative of a group of unusual azaleas native only to the Orient. It is named for a German traveler in the Orient, Baron von Schlippenbach. All in all, it is a superlative plant, and deserves to be more widely used.

The Winterthur Pinetum was planted by Henry Francis du Pont and his father about the time of World War I. Today, a walk through the Pinetum is pleasurable not only for the casual lover of beauty but for the student of plants. Though the aim of Winterthur is not to display complete botanical "collections" of plant families, the Pinetum contains an extensive collection of some of the rarest as well as the most beautiful conifers that can be grown in the eastern United States. Here are the sharp-needled tiger-tail spruce *(Picea polita)*, the dragon spruce *(Picea asperata)*, introduced by E.H.Wilson from China in 1910, and a specimen of the dawn redwood *(Metasequoia glyptostroboides)* which is certainly one of the finest in this country.

The Pinetum always has some special attraction in store for those who stop there. On a hot summer day, one is transported to the cool, shaded galleries of the Pacific rain forests by the pungent resin of giant arborvitaes *(Thuja plicata)*. In spring, stately oriental spruces display an unexpected burst of color in their staminate or male flowers of dark crimson. In early autumn, a kind of premature snowstorm occurs when the abundant cones of Carolina hemlocks *(Tsuga caroliniana)* discharge their pale winged seeds by the thousands. And through autumn, winter, and early spring, this place is a haven for rare grosbeaks, siskins, and crossbills—birds that feed on the seeds of conifers and seldom venture far from the evergreen forests of the far North.

Blooming shrubs and herbaceous plants do, however, add to the beauties of the Pinetum. One of the big spring displays occurs here: the opening of the salmon, pink, white, apricot, and dazzling scarlet flowering quinces that grow along the Chaenomeles Walk.

Royal Azalea. *Rhododendron Schlippenbachi*

Chaenomeles Walk through Pinetum

Early-flowering azaleas of many kinds also bloom throughout the Pinetum. At the south-west edge, huge old crab apples blossom in banks of white, pink, or mauve, and in bays between the evergreens are the new, mammoth-flowered Exbury azaleas and hybrid lilies which bloom in late spring and in summer. One of the most charming walks in the whole garden winds through the crab apples, a path which Mr. du Pont calls his "Once-a-week Path." Along the edges of the Once-a-week Path are planted species and cultivars of azaleas chosen according to their season of bloom, the earliest at the beginning, and the later cultivars farther along the path. The result is that a new azalea opens here once every week during the season (late April to mid-June), and color advances along the walk with the season.

Close to the beginning of the Once-a-week Path are several plants of the pale pink (or white in the clone 'White Find') pinkshell azalea, *Rhododendron Vaseyi*. This native of our southern states somewhat resembles and is as hardy as *R. Schlippenbachi*, and blooms early in May. It is accompanied by drifts of the icy blue spring starflower, *Triteleia uniflora*, a small spring bulb that is aptly named, for its flowers look like stars sprinkled on the

Spring Starflower.
Triteleia uniflora

spring grass. It is a native of Peru and Argentina, and is one of the very few South American bulbs hardy enough to survive out of doors in the United States. It is reported to be satisfactory as far north as New York City.

Triteleia uniflora is, in its classification, one of the most controversial bulbs. It has been shifted from genus to genus of the lily family, including *Triteleia,* and certain authorities today consider it distinct enough to warrant a genus of its own, *Ipheion.* All these genera, moreover, are thought by some to be more closely related to the amaryllises than to the lilies, and have accordingly been removed from the *Liliaceae* and placed in the *Amaryllidaceae.* It seems best at this juncture to list the spring starflower under the name by which it is most commonly known. It may, however, be found in catalogues under an older name, *Brodiaea uniflora,* or even under *Ipheion uniflorum.* By any name it is a lovely thing.

The principal blooming shrubs in Winterthur's old croquet court—now the western portion of the Sundial Garden—are cherries and lilacs. The cherries include the upright Japanese cultivar 'Amanogowa,' with large pink flowers, and the new American hybrid 'Hally Jolivette,' with pale pink flowers and a dense, moundlike habit of growth. The lilacs are all French "Hyacinthiflora" cultivars—hybrids between the common lilac, **Syringa vulgaris,** and the broadleaf lilac, *S. oblata.* These hybrids are in the mauve, mauve-pink, and lavender range of colors, and are similar in every way to the common lilac except that they are a trifle taller and more vigorous, and, more importantly, they bloom a week or ten days earlier.

83

Alabama Fothergilla. *F. monticola*

Near the steps which separate the croquet court from the tennis court areas are golden currant plants, *Ribes aureum,* and small-leaved, mauve, hybrid rhododendrons, a combination echoing the yellow-mauve display of winter-hazel and Korean rhododendron that comes a week or two earlier on the Corylopsis-Mucronulatum Walk.

Beyond the hedge of dwarf box which marks the boundary of the Sundial Garden is a group of native shrubs: the Carolina silverbell, *Halesia carolina,* with drooping white bell-flowers in late April, and *Fothergilla monticola* and *F. major* with fuzzy, creamy white flowers. In *Fothergilla* we have first-rate native ornamentals that are often neglected for inferior exotic material. Like many American plants, they seem to be more appreciated in England, where they were grown by the celebrated physician-naturalist John Fothergill (1712–80) in the middle of the eighteenth century. They are native to swamps and wet pinelands of the Southeast, where they are commonly called "witch-alder." In cultivation they are satisfactory from coastal New England southward, but are not recommended for areas in which winter temperatures fall much lower than ten degrees below zero. Though found in wetlands in the wild, in cultivation they grow quite well in ordinary garden soils. Mildly acid, humus-rich soil suits them best—such soil as azaleas thrive in. They are, incidentally, superb companion plants for early azaleas and rhododendrons, their creamy, bottle-brush blooms making a perfect foil for the more definite shapes and colors of the azalea flowers.

Fothergillas flower in late April. The two species at Winterthur are very similar in appearance, the chief difference being that the bloom spikes of *F. major* are globular while

Fothergillas and Crab Apples

those of *F. monticola* are more elongated and cylindrical. Both grow ultimately to a height of six or eight feet, and both have attractive, witch-hazel-like foliage that turns a brilliant orange or wine red in autumn. They are slow-growing but permanent shrubs, requiring no pruning and little care when once established. They belong to the witch-hazel family, *Hamamelidaceae.*

Another excellent vista at Winterthur is the view from the Sundial Garden in which the "Lookout" on Viburnum Hill is framed between blossom-laden branches of the lilac-lavender princess tree *(Paulownia tomentosa)* and the white Glenn Dale hybrid azalea 'Treasure.' The princess tree (also called empress tree) is named for Anna Pavlovna, the daughter of Czar Paul I of Russia, and, later, Princess of the Netherlands. A tree that occasionally reaches a height of fifty feet, it is unusual in that it is one of the few woody members of the *Scrophulariaceae,* a family composed mainly of herbaceous plants such as foxgloves and snapdragons. The flowers of *Paulownia,* borne in upright panicles on leafless branches in May, resemble those of its relative, the foxglove, except that they are a clear bluish lilac in color. It is not a rare tree—it has in fact become naturalized in many places in this country—yet it is rare enough to provoke questions as to its identity. "How did you ever get a wisteria to grow that big?" a visitor once asked.

The leaves of the princess tree are immense; often two feet in length, they are roughly heart-shaped and pale green. They have no autumn color, remaining green until blackened by the first hard frost. Interesting in winter are both next year's flower buds, fully formed and covered with a rusty felt, and last year's seed capsules, which are prized for use in dried arrangements. The princess tree is a native of China and Japan, and is hardy in this country through most of Zone 4 and southward. Any soil and situation seem to suit it, and it becomes a weed in some areas.

In addition to framing the vista shown here, the paulownias at Winterthur echo the lavender-blue shades of the many lilacs in the Sundial Garden; they lift the color into the air, as it were, and carry it across the road toward the ancient Sycamore, where a large group of mauve redbud, and lavender and mauve azaleas are in bloom in late April and early May.

The yellowhorn, *Xanthoceras sorbifolium,* never fails to move visitors to both admiration and perplexity when it blooms in the Sundial Garden in early May. "Beautiful!" they exclaim, "but what is it?" or, "Lovely! Where can I get one?" And all too often they write later that their nursery "doesn't stock it and never heard of it." For the mystery of the yellowhorn is that it is at the same time one of the most beautiful of flowering trees and one of the most rare. It is not difficult to grow, for it is seldom bothered by diseases, and it thrives in almost any well drained soil. It does, however, require a few years after planting to reach blooming size. It does not root readily from stem cuttings, but can be propagated from seed and from root cuttings, and a few nurserymen in this country who specialize in rare plants offer it for sale. It is worth almost any effort to acquire it.

In early May, just as the lilacs begin to fade, the yellowhorn comes into its own, erupting in large spikes of creamy white flowers among the pale green of unfolding leaves. Each individual flower is about three-fourths of an inch wide, with five cream-white petals and a burnt-orange center. Its summer attractions are finely cut foliage (similar to that of the mountain-ash) and green, walnut-sized fruits. In winter its deeply furrowed brown bark is distinctive. Though seldom exceeding fifteen feet in height, it is treelike rather than shrubby in growth. It usually has a single heavy trunk rather than many slender stems, and it almost never sprouts sucker growth from the base, as do many woody plants of comparable size. The lines of the yellowhorn are always pleasing and restrained; pruning and shaping are rarely needed.

Xanthoceras (it rhymes with rhinoceros) is Greek for "yellow horn," a reference to the

Princess Tree and Azalea. *Paulownia tomentosa* and *Rhododendron* cv. 'Treasure'

Yellowhorn.
Xanthoceras sorbifolium

tiny yellow protrusions deep in the center of each flower; *sorbifolium* is Latin for "with leaves of *Sorbus* (or mountain-ash)," a good description of the foliage. The plant, which is hardy through most of Zone 4 and southward, hails from northern China and is one of the few winter-hardy members of the largely tropical soapberry family, *Sapindaceae*. A close relative, also an excellent ornamental, is the golden-rain tree, *Koelreuteria paniculata* (pages 155-6).

To many people who have visited Winterthur, the name means azaleas. And indeed, azaleas are the most widely used plants at Winterthur, for they are spectacular in color and excellent in foliage and habit. They are planted throughout the gardens, but one section is truly theirs—the "Azalea Woods."

The history of this area is interesting; in a sense it owes its existence to a great disaster. Shortly after the turn of this century, the dreaded chestnut blight spread into Delaware, and killed the massive American chestnuts which, with beech, oak, and tulip-trees, had clothed the Winterthur hills. By 1920, the dense woodland at the crest of the hill north of the house was scarred by open spaces where stands of dead chestnut had been removed. It was here that Mr. du Pont decided to start a nursery for the young azaleas propagated from stock of the first Kurume (pronounced "koo-roo-may") hybrids to appear in this country. These young plants were set in "to fill the gaps" as Mr. du Pont phrased it, but in time they began to do much more. As they grew and bloomed, his eye started matching, blending, and contrasting colors, and he began to see the great potential of these

Yellowhorn.
*Xanthoceras
sorbifolium*

plants in a naturalistic landscape. Beds were enlarged, new beds were made, and paths were cut between beds to permit easy access to the plants. Gradually azaleas came to populate most of the woodland. The "nursery" was fast becoming a garden in its own right.

At all times, however, emphasis remained on the naturalistic. The good gardener may manipulate nature, but he never flouts her. Weedy underbrush was cut out, but desirable natives like *Viburnum pubescens* and flowering dogwood were encouraged to grow. Ferns and wildflowers already grew in abundance in the woodland, but still more, both native and exotic, were planted. Then, in the 1930's the finishing touch was added. Mr. du Pont acquired several flats of seedling rhododendrons from the famous breeder, Charles O. Dexter, of Sandwich, Massachusetts. These were added to the "nursery," and moved about as they bloomed, until gradually they all occupied their final locations. Thus the Azalea Woods slowly took shape, and thus a natural disaster inspired one of the finest horticultural displays in the United States.

Recent additions to the Azalea Woods have been more in the nature of embellishments than changes. Typical are new hybrid rhododendrons, or newly discovered forms of species, such as *Rhododendron vernicosum* (aff. 18139 Rock). The name and number identify this plant as coming from a group of seeds acquired by the great plant collector, J. F. Rock. Fully hardy at Winterthur, it is a superb form of the lacquer rhododendron, with peach-apricot flowers four inches wide in early May. Other additions have been the hybrids 'Goldfort' and 'China,' and several of the newest and showiest of Joseph Gable's hybrids.

Lacquer Rhododendron.
R. vernicosum

But the Dexter hybrids are still the main attraction among rhododendrons. Typical is the brilliant salmon-pink clone shown in the color plate, which is at its peak with the Kurume and torch azaleas in early May. Until the Dexter hybrids appeared, nearly all rhododendrons grown in the East were hybrids of the native *Rhododendron catawbiense* (most of them produced in England nearly a hundred years ago). This species produces admirably hardy and adaptable offspring in which its own purplish magenta color is dominant. These old hybrids, known as the "ironclads" by rhododendron enthusiasts, were in their day fine plants. They still are fine, but their color falls mainly in the purple range, and even those that approach pink and red are somewhat flawed by bluish undertones. Eastern gardeners who saw the multitude of brilliantly colored but tender Asiatic rhododendrons grown in England and on our own West Coast dreamed of having such plants flower in their own gardens. Unfortunately, however, eastern winters proved too severe for anything but the Catawba rhododendron and its descendants.

But one Asiatic species was hardier than most: *R. Fortunei,* named after its discoverer, the English plant hunter, Robert Fortune. It differed from the familiar Catawba hybrids in many ways: it had larger flowers in a looser truss; it was fragrant; it bloomed earlier; and, most importantly, its color varied from pale pink to ivory white, with no blue in it at all. With a few of its close relatives, it became the basis of the Dexter hybrids, which are only now becoming well known in the gardening world. These plants are not so hardy as the Catawbas, but many do well in Boston, and an especially hardy group is bred in

Ohio. They bloom as a rule two weeks earlier than the Catawbas, and their colors do not conflict with these plants at all. Some of their colors were new in eastern rhododendrons: true bright pink, blush pink, salmon, apricot, and cherry red, all free from the blue undertones that flaw most Catawbas. As with other plants, the best clones on the market are named varieties. Most plants sold simply as "Dexter hybrids" are unselected seedlings, and nearly always prove to be of indifferent quality. Some of the finest of the named clones in commerce today are the apricot 'Skyglow,' the clear lavender 'Amethyst,' the pink 'Brookville,' the bright pink 'Scintillation,' and the sparkling cerise-pink 'Mrs. W. R. Coe.'

From the original Dexter seedlings which flowered at Winterthur, about sixty were selected as good plants (inferior seedlings were discarded), and given identifying numbers. All are excellent, and a few are really outstanding. One of these is Winterthur Dexter Hybrid No. 1 (so numbered because it is usually the first of the lot to bloom), which has large flat flowers of salmon with a definite orange undertone. Another is No. 6, with flowers of a soft biscuit yellow—a totally distinct and lovely color—and good foliage and growth habits, two attributes which are often missing from rhododendrons in the yellow class. This clone has been registered with the American Rhododendron Society under the name 'Tan.' A third hybrid, as good as any in commerce, is No. 11, a clear, brilliant cherry red with a rather dwarf habit of growth and excellent deep green, pointed leaves.

Countless native wildflowers were planted in the Azalea Woods to supplement those already growing there: *Viola papilionacea,* the common blue violet; the blue and white *V. Priceana;* the cream *V. striata;* and two yellow violets, *V. eriocarpa* and *V. pubescens.* Other natives planted were wild blue phlox, trilliums, bloodroot, rue-anemone, jack-in-the-pulpit, Jacob's-ladder, and Virginia bluebells. Ferns of several species were introduced, and, in addition, many woodland wildflowers from other countries were naturalized among the natives. Today English primroses bloom with American trilliums; European periwinkle and wild phlox from the hills of Pennsylvania mingle their lavender blossoms; blue Eurasian squills and chionodoxas carpet the floor of the woodland, and are followed by the blue of *Mertensia* dug from the banks of the Brandywine.

Noteworthy in a collection of notable plants is a foreigner that stands alone: the torch azalea, *Rhododendron Kaempferi,* native to the high slopes of Mount Fujiyama in Japan. The tallest and one of the two hardiest cultivated azaleas in the Obtusum sub-series (the conventional "evergreen" azaleas), the torch azalea is almost completely deciduous, and, unlike most of the closely related Kurume hybrids, is upright and open in habit, eventually reaching a height of ten or twelve feet. At Winterthur it occupies a large section of the Azalea Woods near the entrance path, where it blooms above the wild violets, phlox, and periwinkle very early in May, slightly before the Kurume hybrids.

Some plants are so tall that visitors can stand beneath their blossom-laden branches. *R. Kaempferi* is as floriferous as any azalea, and seems even more so because at blooming time it has no foliage at all. The color of the torch azalea varies from clear salmon pink to vibrant salmon red. It does best in a partially shaded position; its flowers fade quickly in very hot sun. Fully hardy at the Arnold Arboretum in Boston (whence the first plants at Winterthur came not long after their introduction from Japan in 1892), it is dependable throughout Zone 6 and in sheltered spots in Zone 5. Its specific name commemorates Engelbert Kaempfer, a German traveler-explorer in the Orient. Some botanists regard it as a variety of the Kirishima azalea, *R. obtusum;* thus it is often offered in nursery lists as *R. obtusum Kaempferi.*

Wildflowers are usually thought of as helpers, as plants that enhance rather than make an effect. But at Winterthur there is a bed of wildflowers, great white trilliums *(Trillium grandiflorum),* which is a spectacle in itself. The plants inhabit an open area in the center of the Azalea Woods which is surrounded by brilliantly blooming azaleas and rhododen-

Bluebells in Azalea Woods. *Scilla campanulata*

drons, yet not one visitor fails to pause and comment on the trilliums' beautiful effect.

The great white trillium (also known as the snow trillium, showy trillium, or large-flowered trillium) is the showiest species of the genus, and the dominant species at Winterthur. Gray's *Manual of Botany* describes it as "our handsomest, most fickle and sporting species, with many scores of aberrant forms described." Only one of these aberrant forms grows at Winterthur, and it is perhaps even more beautiful than the species. It is *forma petalosum,* in which stamens and carpels have been modified into petals, producing the effect of a pure white, double camellia on a conventional trillium plant. Since this form has no sexual parts, it must be increased by division alone, and is therefore still quite uncommon in gardens. Only a few rare plant nurseries handle it.

Trillium grandiflorum is native to the whole eastern half of our continent. Though extremely rare in its wild state on the Delmarva Peninsula, it does thrive under woodland conditions in Delaware. It is more than a curiosity or a connoisseur's plant; it is an outstanding ornamental in its own right. Its three-petaled white flowers, which turn a pleasing rose pink as they age, last nearly a month, from late April to late May. A member of the lily family, *Liliaceae,* it is, like all trilliums, distinct in having its floral parts arranged in threes: there are three large white petals, three smaller green sepals, and a whorl of three green leaves surrounding the flowers. *Trillium* is from the Latin for triple, an allusion to this tripartite structure.

Other trilliums at Winterthur (in the Trillium Bed and scattered through the woodland) include the purple trillium or wakerobin, *T. erectum,* a tall, vigorous species with flowers of deep maroon, and *T. cernuum,* the nodding trillium, a graceful but not very showy species with small white flowers partially hidden beneath its leaves. Very distinct is the yellow toadshade trillium, *T. sessile luteum,* a native of the southern mountains, which grows happily in one corner of the Trillium Bed. In this species the flowers are rather small and stalkless ("sessile" is the botanical term), that is, set right down in the whorl of leaves. They are also unusual in that their pale yellow petals are upright rather than spreading. The three broad leaves are attractively marbled with grayish tones and dark green, and are the plant's chief claim to showiness. Although odd rather than beautiful, it is a plant that visitors always notice.

The main show of the Azalea Woods, however, is neither wildflowers nor rhododendrons—it is azaleas, huge in size, lavish in color, overwhelming in abundance of bloom. In dozens of places along the paths through the wood one can look about and see nothing on all sides but tall trees, flowering dogwoods, and drift upon drift of azaleas. Nearly all the azaleas in the Azalea Woods are Kurume hybrids, derivatives of *Rhododendron obtusum* developed by breeders near the little town of Kurume in Japan, and first brought to this country for exhibition at the San Francisco Exposition in 1915. Kurume azaleas are distinguished by a dense, compact habit of growth and by comparatively small flowers produced so abundantly that they completely cover the plant. Their blooming time in Delaware is the first two weeks in May. Most are quite evergreen in mild climates, but lose a good part of their leaves in colder areas. They are hardy from Zone 6 southward, but in the northern part of their range they should be planted in sites protected from winter sun and wind. These azaleas are excellent for even the smallest gardens, for they are compact in growth, attractive even when out of bloom, and they flower when only a few inches high. The most widely known Kurume cultivar is probably 'Hinodegiri,' the brilliant crimson azalea so often planted in front of houses in this country—and, all too often, jarringly against red brick.

The Kurume azaleas at Winterthur include many colors. They have been here so long that many of the names have been lost. Some of the best named azaleas are the bright pink double 'Pink Pearl,' the pale pink double 'Cherry Blossom,' the double white 'Snow,'

Bed of Great White Trillium. *T. grandiflorum*

The Azalea Woods

and the shimmering pink 'Hino-Mayo.' Others, now known simply by numbers, are of various colors: deep rose, white, white with mauve stripes, solid mauve, salmon, and cherry red. The whites are used abundantly to tone down and blend the brighter colors since the color of most Kurume azaleas is remarkable for its clarity and brilliance. The ever present difficulty in landscaping with azaleas lies in obtaining maximum intensity of color without completely overwhelming the eye. At Winterthur, the trees, wildflowers, and specimen rhododendrons diminish this intensity, as do the canopy of white dogwood, the abundance of white azaleas, and the actual distribution and blending of the more brightly colored azaleas. For example, the reds are for the most part planted with whites, or isolated at the edge of the woodland. Sombre or unemphatic colors, which provide relief from brighter hues, are massed in strategic spots: one bed is composed entirely of white varieties; another consists entirely of varieties in different shades of mauve. Finally, many subtle combinations of tones seduce the eye. An extremely effective example is the juxtaposition of a pale mauve clone and a cherry-red clone (the *amoenum* × *Kaempferi* hybrid, 'Arnoldiana'). Here the mauve clone makes the crimson seem clearer and brighter, and the crimson makes the mauve seem almost a cool lavender blue in contrast. This combination appears again and again: in the group of crimson azalea 'Hexe' and mauve *Rhododendron carolinianum* on the walk from the Azalea Woods to the Pinetum; in the planting of mixed crimson-red azaleas and the lavender-mauve Gable azalea 'Viola' on the path

96

from the Sundial Garden to the Bristol Summerhouse; and, very early in June, in the blending of mauve *Buddleia alternifolia* and crimson *Weigela* cv. 'Eva Rathke' under the princess trees near the Sundial Garden.

An even more subtle blending of colors occurs in the Azalea Woods in a great drift of pink azaleas composed of three distinct cultivars—a double deep pink (No. 10), a double medium pink ('Pink Pearl'), and a double pale pink ('Cherry Blossom'). Though these are planted in apparently random fashion throughout the bed, in reality the deepest shade is massed at one end and the palest at the other, with the medium shade in between. Intermingling of individual plants, however, eliminates any suggestion of distinct bands of color, and the visual effect is a gradual shift from light to deep pink. The three varieties differ only in intensity, not in hue; that is, all three are shades of true pink. This is important, for were they not different saturations of a single color, they would not blend so readily. If one were, say, salmon or mauve pink, the effect would be that of two distinct colors—and probably two distinct colors that harmonize poorly. Worst of all, if one were salmon, and another that shade of pink with a blue undertone that is common in azaleas (Mr. du Pont's term "blue pink" is probably the most accurate description of this peculiar color), the effect would probably be unpleasant; the salmon would look brassy and the "blue pink" harsh and grating.

An abundance of anything begins eventually to cloy, even (or perhaps especially) an abundance of beautiful color. The azaleas at Winterthur would be overpowering if they were planted in the open. In the Azalea Woods, however, the dark massiveness of towering trees balances the flood of color below, and on the ground also are sights that afford the eye temporary rest and refreshment. Among these are the cool green pitchers of jack-in-the-pulpit, *Arisaema triphyllum*. The "flower" of this native plant immediately identifies it as a member of the arum family, *Araceae*, a close relative of both the lowly skunk cabbage of woodland bogs and the elegant calla of florists' shops. The so-called flower of all aroids is actually a group of many tiny flowers clustered on a clublike organ, the *spadix* (the "jack" of jack-in-the-pulpit, and the yellow "finger" in the calla), which is partially enveloped by an often brightly colored, modified leaf, the *spathe* (the "pulpit" of our woodland friend, and what is usually thought of as the flower of the calla). As each tiny flower on the spadix is fertilized, it forms a fleshy berry, which in *Arisaema triphyllum* is brilliant scarlet. The cylindrical mass of these scarlet berries is very showy in late summer and autumn.

Other names for this familiar plant are Indian-turnip and, in French Canada, "wild onion" and "little preacher." It grows from an underground tuber which allegedly was part of the diet of the early Indians. Anyone planning to add it to his, however, should be warned that all aroids contain irritants in their sap in the form of microscopic crystals of calcium oxalate which painfully irritate the mouth. *Dieffenbachia*, the popular houseplant commonly called "dumb cane" or "mother-in-law plant," is an aroid that inherits its common names from these irritant crystals, which cause numbness and even a kind of paralysis of the mouth. Heat breaks up the crystals, however, so that tubers of *Arisaema triphyllum* are edible when properly cooked. Poi, the ancient staple diet of Hawaii—as all crossword puzzle fans know—is made from a tuber of this family.

China is the home of some of the most beautiful rhododendrons on earth. They grow there in an abundance and a diversity unequaled in any other region; the great *Fortunei* series, of which *Rhododendron Fortunei* is the type species, is centered there. This series of beautiful and comparatively hardy rhododendrons includes several which are among the earliest in the genus to flower.

In 1946 Mr. du Pont purchased from the Dexter estate twenty-four plants of one of these species, *R. praevernum*, originally from the Hupeh province of central China. *R. praevernum*

Jack-in-the-Pulpit.
Arisaema triphyllum

(*praevernum* in Latin means "before the spring") is known as the "February rhododendron" for the month in which it supposedly blooms in its native land. In America, at least on the East Coast, it seldom blooms before April. But when in bloom it is spectacular, with its flat-topped clusters of bright pink buds and paler pink bell-shaped flowers lighting up the gaunt, wintry woodland in which it grows. The plants at Winterthur bloom every year about the first week of April, a period when days may be as balmy as June and nights as frigid as January. To protect the blossoms from late frosts, burlap is stretched on frames above the plants.

R.praevernum has somehow become confused in the trade with two of its close relatives, *R. fargesii* and *R. oreodoxa*. But since all three are closely similar in appearance, blooming date, and hardiness, this confusion is understandable. All are satisfactory in the East at least as far north as Long Island, and all are completely dependable in the "Rhododen-dron Belt" of the West Coast.

Rivaling the Trillium Bed in showiness is another group of herbaceous plants in the Azalea Woods, a carpet of blue and white anemones which raise their daisy-like heads and sway with every breeze in late April and early May. Some are sky blue, others white, the rest every shade in between.

Mr. du Pont reports that these plants appeared spontaneously in the Azalea Woods many years ago. How they got here is a mystery; perhaps a few tubers were buried in the soil ball of one of the shrubs purchased and planted in the area. They are apparently

February Rhododendron. *R. praevernum*

happy in their location, for they have increased their numbers many times over. These are Italian windflowers, *Anemone appenina*, the counterpart in Italy of the Greek *A. blanda*. The Italian plant resembles its Greek relative, and thrives under the same culture. It differs in that it is taller and perhaps a bit more vigorous, and lacks the bright yellow "eye" which is so prominent in the center of the flower of *A. blanda*. In addition it blooms almost a month later.

May provides spectacle on spectacle in the Azalea Woods—orange-pink masses of torch azalea; blue sheets of anemone; white expanses of trillium; multicolored drifts of azaleas; the splendor of each rhododendron—enough color to glut the most color-hungry eye. Nor is beauty on a smaller scale lacking: the tiny rue-anemones on stems of thread; the white-petaled bloodroots, miniature waterlilies one day and shattered the next; the Virginia bluebells whose arching spikes of pink buds open amazingly into pure blue flowers. And then there is the kind of beauty appreciated intellectually rather than visually—the beauty of the drab oak flower that will be acorn, of the green spikes of lily flowers that will blaze in summer, of the unrolling fronds of young ferns.

No words, no photographs however fine, can convey the total attraction of the Azalea Woods. It must be experienced firsthand. A final element of the total picture must be mentioned, however—people. Visitors, often as gaily bedecked as the flowers they have come to see, are an overlooked attraction of Winterthur. For those of us who have become familiar with the place, for whom the plants have become old faces, the exclamations of those seeing it for the first time rekindle old wonder. We see afresh what we have come to take for granted. What a waste Winterthur would be if it flowered and passed away unseen!

> *"But when the melancholy fit shall fall*
> *Sudden from heaven like a weeping cloud,*
> *That fosters the droop-headed flowers all,*
> *And hides the green hill in an April shroud;*
> *Then glut thy sorrow on a morning rose,*
> *Or on the rainbow of the salt sand-wave,*
> *Or on the wealth of globèd peonies..."*

So says John Keats in his "Ode on Melancholy." And perhaps only Keats, whose appreciation of earthly beauty was heightened by the awareness of his imminent death, could with the one word "wealth" so accurately characterize peonies. For peonies do indeed possess a richness, an abundance, a sheer extravagance of splendor equaled by no other flower.

But melancholia is by no means prerequisite to a visit to Winterthur's Peony Garden. The cheerful will leave this place feeling even more cheerful, for it is one of Winterthur's finest floral displays. It is also one of the most recent; in its finished form it dates only from about 1953, though some of the plants have been growing here for over eighty years. Today it consists of beds of herbaceous peonies and groups of tree peonies laid out on a slope divided by steps into three levels and bisected by a path. It is one of the least naturalistic sections of the garden, for the nature of peonies precludes naturalistic planting; accordingly, there is a great deal of garden architecture in the area. Flanking the steps between the highest and middle levels are white "beehives" from Latimeria, and opposite these, at the far edge of the middle level, is a latticed summerhouse, also from Latimeria. Counteracting the somewhat artificial tone of these structures are the surroundings—tall beeches and other forest trees, and conifers such as feathery false-cypresses—and other less formal plants among the peonies themselves. Those that bloom with the peonies

Italian Windflower. *Anemone appenina*

include mauve Persian lilac, coral Tatarian honeysuckle, pink beauty-bush, mauve-pink late lilac, and lavender-blue clematis 'Ramona.'

The *Ranunculaceae*, which includes peonies, is a family of beautiful plants. It contains the showy turban ranunculus and poppy anemone of florists, as well as such garden treasures as the windflower, buttercup, Christmas-rose, marsh-marigold, hepatica, adonis, aconite, winter-aconite, larkspur, meadow-rue, columbine, and clematis. *Paeonia* is perhaps the showiest genus in this showy family. In the United States, peonies are represented almost entirely by the big, double Chinese peonies that bloom at the end of May and are widely used for cemetery decoration on Memorial Day. The Chinese peonies are all clones of a single species, *Paeonia albiflora,* just one of the twenty-five or so species of peony in the world. Until recently, there were very few peony hybrids on the market, but now, due to the work of a few enterprising hybridizers, many fine and entirely distinct new plants are finding acceptance among American gardeners.

None of the peonies at Winterthur are conventional peonies. They are all Saunders hybrids, produced by Professor A.P. Saunders of Clinton, New York, who was unquestionably the outstanding pioneer in peony breeding. Scouring the world to find species to use in his breeding program, Professor Saunders acquired plants such as the fern-leaved crimson *P. tenuifolia* from eastern Europe, the delicate *P. Emodii* from the Himalayas, and the rare sulphur yellow *P. Mlokosewitschii* from the Caucasus. From crosses of these and other species, he evolved a race—or rather several races—of distinct and charming peony hybrids. Most of these are single or semi-double, but are fully as showy as the double Chinese peonies, and possess a grace unknown in the latter plants. The white, pink, and beet red colors of the old-fashioned peonies have been expanded in the new hybrids to include ivory, yellow, pinks so brilliant that they fairly shout, pinks that approach salmon, cerise, or lavender, true scarlet reds, and blended shades with the texture of mother-of-pearl.

At the same time the blooming season has been expanded. Whereas the old-fashioned peonies bloom each year around Memorial Day (or later in the North), most of the new hybrids bloom much earlier. The earliest of all is 'Daystar,' a hybrid of *P. Mlokosewitschii* with single yellow flowers appearing the first week in May. This plant is a triumph of the breeder's art. Its gorgeous blossoms, resembling mammoth buttercups, have to be seen to be believed. Others follow close on 'Daystar': the double white 'Camellia,' which in form of flower closely resembles its namesake; the bright salmon-pinks 'Janice,' 'Gillian,' and 'Grace Root'; the deep rose 'Ludovica'; the scarlet 'Red Red Rose'; the huge single whites, 'Winterthur' and 'Big White'; and two 'Windflowers,' one early and the other a slightly later hybrid of *P. Emodii*, both of which have small, single white flowers on long, graceful stems, and look more like large anemones than peonies.

Many more Saunders hybrid peonies might be mentioned here, but peonies of other types demand attention. Three species of peony are shrubby rather than herbaceous; that is, they do not die to the ground in winter but continue to grow each year until they reach a height of six feet or so. These are called "tree" peonies, and of these three, by far the most important is the Chinese Moutan, *Paeonia suffruticosa*, which has been cultivated so long in the Orient that the wild type is virtually lost. The color range of the Moutan includes dark reds, shades of pink and purple, and white. It blooms in Delaware about the middle of May. In cultivation there are two general types: those developed in China, which have immense double flowers, often a foot across, and those developed in Japan, which, as one might expect from Japan, are smaller, with single or semi-double flowers.

Countless varieties of Moutan have been introduced into cultivation, and nearly all are outstanding ornamental shrubs. Perhaps the finest is a cultivar known as 'Gessekai,' a tall, vigorous white which somehow combines extremely large size and showiness with ethereal loveliness. Not quite so ethereal, but immensely showy are the light pinks 'Kin-Tagio' and

Saunders Tree Peony. *Paeonia* cv. 'Chinese Dragon'

The Peony Garden

'Tama-Fuyo,' the huge deeper pink 'Shin-Tenchi,' the double dark red 'Uba-Tama,' and the big double blush pink 'Yae-Zakura,' whose name means "very double cherry blossom."

The two other shrubby species of peony, also natives of China, appear never to have been cultivated in that country. This is puzzling, for one species, *P. lutea*, has blossoms of pure yellow, the imperial color of China, and a color unknown in other tree peonies and, indeed, in most other peonies. The flowers of *P. Delavayi*, a low, rather scrubby species, are a deep blackish maroon. Soon after these two species were cultivated in Europe and America, a few far-sighted individuals began crossing them with *P. suffruticosa* in an attempt to combine the large flowers and robust constitution of the latter with the unusual colors of the former. It was not an easy cross to make; a discouraging number of attempts ended in failure, and those that did not fail invariably produced sterile progeny, thus precluding further improvement through hybridization of the offspring. Such was the beauty of both parents, however, that most of the crosses produced good, ornamental garden plants in just one generation.

The two great names in this field are those of Lemoine and, again, Saunders. Lemoine, a nurseryman of Nancy, France, who made his reputation in many areas of horticulture, crossed *P. lutea* with the double Chinese cultivars of *P. suffruticosa*, producing such varieties as 'Alice Harding,' 'Chromatella,' 'L'Espérance,' 'La Lorraine,' and 'Souvenir de Maxime Cornu,' all of which have yellow, or red and yellow flowers. The one great flaw in most of the Lemoine varieties is that they have inherited the double flowers of their Moutan parent and the stem of *P. lutea*, with the result that the flowers, too heavy for their slender stems, droop and are hidden in the foliage. Individual blooms are superb as cut flowers,

Moutan Tree Peony.
Paeonia suffruticosa cv.
'Yae-Zakura'

but the plants suffer as ornamentals because of the drooping flowers. The last two varieties mentioned, both full doubles and both, unfortunately, droopers, have been growing at Winterthur for more than forty years.

Professor Saunders was active in breeding tree peonies as well as herbaceous types. He had the sagacity to use as parents the single and semi-double cultivars of *P. suffruticosa*, for none of his creations, even those that are double, possess the faults of the Lemoine hybrids. The Saunders tree peonies are glorious garden subjects: tall, vigorous plants with large flowers of red, black maroon, blended mauve, buff, amber, and pure, breathtaking yellow. They are little known and rather expensive, for tree peonies are slow and difficult to propagate, which, more than any other factor, has prevented their becoming popular. Probably the best known and least expensive is 'Argosy,' a clear yellow single. More costly are: 'Canary,' a bright yellow single and one of the finest; 'Age of Gold,' a double yellow; 'Apricot' and 'Countess,' both "tea rose" blends of rose and buff yellow; 'Mystery' and 'Princess,' both an odd, blended, pearly mauve pink; 'Chinese Dragon,' a big, flashy red; 'Daredevil,' a single deep garnet; 'Vesuvian,' a double deep garnet; and the single 'Black Pirate' and double 'Black Douglas,' both *Delavayi* hybrids of intense black maroon. All these and many more bloom in the Peony Garden at Winterthur, flowering a week or ten days later than the *suffruticosa* cultivars, and thus extending the tree peony season.

It is difficult to convey the spectacle that tree peonies of either type make. Some idea of their size and showiness can be suggested by the fact that more than one visitor coming

on them for the first time has thought momentarily that he was seeing dahlias blooming in May. They are so beautiful that most people look instinctively for a hidden flaw, else why are they not more popular? They must be tender, difficult to grow, disease-prone—something. Not so. They are really no more difficult than herbaceous peonies, and they require almost the same cultural conditions. Like other peonies, they do well in rich, well drained loamy soil which is neutral or slightly alkaline in reaction, and they appreciate watering during summer droughts. A summer mulch of well rotted manure, and an occasional liming are beneficial, but mulching material should be removed during the winter since it tends to harbor disease organisms. As to hardiness, they are ironclad throughout much of this country, thriving in most of Zones 4, 5, 6, 7, and 8. Like other peonies, they do best undisturbed, although they recover quickly after transplanting; first-year grafted plants a foot high will often bear a single flower almost a foot in diameter. They are extremely long-lived. At Winterthur, three plants of a deep purple clone of *P. suffruticosa*, planted in 1880, still thrive and bloom each year.

Since tree peonies are among the first shrubs to leaf out in spring, it is important that they be sheltered from the east, because on frosty mornings the sun will burn the new foliage and developing flower buds. If they must be planted with an eastern exposure, they may be protected by a burlap screen. However, if they are wrapped with burlap, the new growth is likely to grow through the material and be broken off in the unwrapping unless it is removed very early in the season. Their only really serious enemy is peony botrytis blight, which causes wilting of flowering stems and, ultimately, of whole branches. This may be arrested temporarily by removal of the infected branches, and prevented altogether by two or three applications of a fungicide (such as Bordeaux mixture) at ten-day intervals in early spring.

Here is a spring view of the garden seat we last saw in winter. The gnarled Osage-oranges growing over it have not yet leafed out, but its roof provides shade from the spring sunshine. Beyond it are May-blooming Gable azaleas in shades of wine red and plum purple, rich and deep against the green of lawn and conifers. All around the little seat are bulbs and wildflowers. Spring beauties and tiny English daisies dot the grass with pink and white. Soft blue Spanish bluebells, blue and white periwinkle, violets, and the ubiquitous and intrusive but nevertheless delightful green and white stars-of-Bethlehem (*Ornithogalum umbellatum*) grow in and along the edge of the woodland to the left of the seat.

Here also grows another ornithogalum, not intrusive and not at all ubiquitous, the tall nodding star-of-Bethlehem, *O. nutans*. This unusual plant bears, on foot-high scapes in April, star-shaped flowers that are neither gray nor green nor white, but a soft blend of all three. It is exceedingly graceful in the garden and, because of its distinct coloration, superb for cutting. Patrick Synge, editor of the *Journal of the Royal Horticultural Society*, and author of one of the best books on bulbs, *The Complete Guide to Bulbs*, calls it one of the most beautiful plants in its genus. It is native to southern Europe, but is naturalized in Great Britain and, sparingly, in America. In this country it is most often seen around abandoned farmhouses, where it persists for many years. I have dug from such stands bulbs which were well over a foot beneath the turf. No doubt this great depth insures the bulbs' survival against grazing cows, rooting pigs, and flower-pulling people. In the garden, the bulbs of this species should be planted about six inches deep, in sun or shade. They will, like daffodils, naturalize easily in grass which is not cut before the first of June.

Ornithogalum, a member of the lily family, is a genus of over a hundred species, all native to Europe. The name, "bird's milk" in Greek, is possibly an allusion to the translucent, egg white flowers of many species, or perhaps it is a reference to the fact that the bulbs of many species are edible. One theory is that the manna eaten by the wandering Israelites was composed in part of the bulbs of an ornithogalum, probably *O. umbellatum*.

Garden Seat

Nodding Star-of-Bethlehem. *Ornithogalum nutans*

Page 59 shows the Museum from the hilltop north of the building, through the bud-laden branches of an early magnolia. Here is the reverse of that view, a photograph taken from the Museum up the hill, just a few days later than the other one. The ancient magnolia, now fully clothed in white, contrasts effectively against the tall, columnar oriental spruce standing behind and slightly to the left of it. In the foreground to the far left is one of the magnificent tulip-trees that add so much to the Winterthur landscape. Here also are oaks, beeches, and various conifers. The time is late April. Precocious blooms appear on the magnolia, and other trees disclose a dozen different shades of green, bronze, and wine red in their opening leaves. Everything is muted, softly colored, flickering with light and shadow. It is one of the most delightful times of the year.

On page 92 is a view of the azaleas just up the hill from the garden seat. The bed includes a few purple-toned Gable azaleas and, on the far left, a group of late-blooming Kaempferi hybrids. The azaleas on the lawn are plants of the well known, brilliant crimson Kurume hybrid 'Hinodegiri,' spectacular here in its setting of green. Just over the hill beyond the 'Hinodegiri' appear the outlines of the Museum. The herbaceous plants in the drift in the foreground are *Scilla campanulata*, Spanish bluebells or wood-hyacinths. This section of the garden contains thousands of these bulbous plants of the lily family. They raise their racemes of soft lavender-blue bells throughout nearly the whole month of May, contrasting first with the early Kurume and Gable azaleas, and later with the flamboyant orange pinks and salmon reds of the late Kaempferi hybrids that line a path to the left.

Rhododendron mucronatum cv. 'Magnifica' with George and Martha Washington Figures

Near the little garden seat is a grass walk that ends in a roofed archway, which, because of its extraordinary roof, has been nicknamed "The Mexican Hat." It is another structure brought from the Latimer estate. The Mexican Hat serves as a focal point for the view down the grass path, and as a backdrop for the magnificent azaleas that line the walk and for the two pieces of metal statuary, figures of George and Martha Washington, standing among the azaleas. These two pieces of Americana are made of hollow metal, and dressed, not in the style of their day, but in the flowing robes of Rome. They originally performed a utilitarian as well as an ornamental function, being ornate stovepipes that helped to hold and distribute heat.

The large-flowered, strawberry-blotched, white azalea surrounding George and Martha brings the size and splendor of the southern Indica azaleas to northern gardens. It is called 'Magnifica,' and it is a form of a very old Japanese garden plant, *Rhododendron mucronatum* (not to be confused with *R. mucronulatum*, a totally different plant), the snow azalea, better known in America by its old names, *Azalea ledifolia alba* and *A. indica alba*. Mystery surrounds the origin of the snow azalea. It is certainly Japanese, for it was found growing abundantly in gardens by the first westerners to visit Japan. But it has never been found in the wild, either in Japan or in the other Oriental countries to which evergreen azaleas are native. It is now thought to be a hybrid, produced perhaps centuries ago in Japan.

Lending support to this theory is the fact that *R. mucronulatum* is an extremely variable plant. The typical form has pure white flowers sometimes three inches broad, blooming in Delaware the second or third week in May. The plant itself is seldom taller than six feet, and is broader than it is tall, bearing gray-green leaves covered with sticky hairs. Its foliage is not so pleasing as that of the glossy-leaved Kurumes, and it is more susceptible to attack by the azalea white fly, which finds the hairy leaves attractive. For size and sheer beauty of flower, however, it cannot be surpassed. Some of the commoner forms of *R. mucronatum* are 'Lilacina,' a taller plant with lavender-mauve blossoms, and 'Sekidera,' white with a rose blotch. The azalea known in the trade as 'Delaware Valley White' is also probably just a clone of *R. mucronatum*.

'Magnifica' is not for some reason common in the trade. It has been declared synonymous with 'Sekidera,' but there is a great difference between the two; the Winterthur 'Magnifica,' at least, is much more showy. 'Magnifica' is rather prone to mutations or sports. Occasional branches will bear blossoms that are completely pink or mauve pink, or sometimes pure mauve. Many years ago one mutation appeared at Winterthur that was a clear, soft lavender in color, and sweetly scented. This was propagated and named 'Winterthur,' and today figures prominently in the gardens. It is especially beautiful when planted alone in the shade of tall trees, where its soft color and sweet fragrance offer a cool respite from the late spring sun.

'Magnifica,' like the rest of the forms of *R. mucronatum,* begins blooming in mid-May, and is showy for the rest of the month. It is a valuable azalea to extend the season, since it blooms a good two weeks later than the Kurume hybrids. It has, at least in the climate of Delaware, the added distinction of being one of the few azaleas with two seasons of bloom, for it continues to open at least a few flowers from early autumn right up until the first frost (see page 168). *R. mucronatum* and its forms are hardy from Zone 6 southward. They are perfectly hardy on Long Island and in protected spots in coastal New England where, reportedly, they bloom earlier than they do in Delaware.

The great genus *Rhododendron* begins and ends the spring season at Winterthur. *Rhododendron mucronulatum* opens its rich mauve blossoms before winter's frosts have ended; the large-leaved *R. discolor* opens its immense, fragrant trumpets in the summery heat of June. Our own native *R. maximum,* though less showy in flower than *R. discolor,* blooms as late as early July in the latitude of Delaware, and many members of the section *Azalea* bloom even later: the native "swamp honeysuckle," *R. viscosum,* opens its flowers throughout June and July, and a southern relative, the plum-leaf azalea *(R. prunifolium),* seldom shows its orange-red blossoms before the middle of July in Delaware. But with the great flush of bloom on azaleas such as 'Magnifica' in late May, spring truly ends. For during this period come days of searing summer heat that wilt the delicate corollas of the azaleas before their time. The squills, snowdrops, even daffodils, that brightened the ground in late winter and early spring are now in full leaf, at the very end of their cycle of growth. Everywhere the swelling seed capsules of summer are replacing the last flowers of spring.

The advance of spring is accompanied by a gradual cessation of bird music as the duties of rearing families replace the earlier activity of staking out territory and building nests. Each morning in March and April the frosty air is split by the bugling of a pair of Canada geese which nest on one Winterthur pond but feed and dawdle on another. Their regular eight a.m. feeding flight resounds with honking. And then one morning in late April they are heard no more. Their brood has hatched, and these usually loud and fearless birds are warily secreting their tender goslings in some remote corner of a pond. Little will be seen or heard of them until the goslings grow stronger and are able to make their debut on the ponds of Winterthur. Finally, they appear as awkward adolescents, nearly as large as their parents, though still clothed in olive-gray down.

Summer

Summer comes trailing after spring: a slow lengthening of the day, a gradual intensification of warmth, the last few flowers still blooming on the mid-season azaleas, a scarcely perceptible slackening of the rhythm of life. On the calendar, the summer solstice occurs on the twenty-first of June, but here the first day of summer falls closer to the first of June. By then, all the flowers that make a festival of spring have fallen or are quickly fading. Lilacs, cherries, and most azaleas are colorless. Discolored flowers are falling from rhododendrons. Bright petals from shattered peonies litter the grass. June days are too warm for the true flowers of spring; their places are taken by more heat-resistant blossoms—mock-orange, deutzia, late lilac and spirea, a few late peonies, rhododendrons and azaleas. These create a kind of backwash in the tide of summer, giving one last burst of bloom before the year moves on into high summer, a period rich with leaf but few blossoms, hot and still with the songs of few birds.

Summer is the seasonal opposite of winter, yet the two are similar in some respects. Spring and fall are the brightest, and summer and winter the drabbest seasons. As the exhilaration of autumn gives way to the weariness of winter, so the freshness of spring becomes tarnished by summer. Flowers wither, dust films the foliage, drought discolors, and insects ravage the leaves of shrubs and trees. The elements oppress us most during winter and summer, and so too do they oppress the garden. Plants that survive winter freezes, the standing water of thaws, and the dead weight of snow may succumb to the heat and drought of summer. Both are seasons of concern for the gardener.

But summer has moments of transcendent beauty. Early summer for me will always be the unearthly song, reverberant and loud almost beyond bearing, of the ovenbird in Chandler Woods. And high summer is remembered not as dusty leaves and faded flowers, but as velvety black and yellow goldfinches feeding among sky blue chicory in the early freshness of an August morning, or a meadow flaming with the orange of butterflyweed, or a cool, damp woodland bejeweled with the ruby spires of cardinalflower of the purest, brightest red imaginable, and attended by iridescent hummingbirds.

Summer-blooming plants are comparatively rare (with the exception of annuals, which have little place in a naturalistic landscape), and summer-blooming shrubs and trees are

Hybrid Lilies and Tamarisks. *Lilium* cv. 'Destiny' and *Tamarix pentandra*   115

especially rare. The gardener who plans a summer garden must exercise considerable ingenuity in order to keep his creation from becoming dull and monotonous. Among shrubs, certain summer standbys such as mock-orange, deutzia, spirea, hydrangea, and rose-of-Sharon may always be depended upon. These, however, are not sufficiently showy to make a summer garden interesting all season long; they must be used with other plants. At Winterthur, for example, late-flowering native azaleas from the southern mountains provide accents of color among white mock-orange. The pink native mountain-laurel blooms with mauve and pink late lilacs. In the woods, *Viburnum pubescens*, with flowers like Queen-Anne's-lace, echoes in subdued but effective fashion the white fountains of deutzia and spirea on Oak Hill. And among the summer shrubs near the old Sycamore are many beds of those most colorful of summer flowers, lilies.

It is most appropriate to begin with the lilies, for they are the constant companions of summer at Winterthur. In June, the upright orange and yellow hybrids derived from *Lilium bulbiferum* and *L.* × *umbellatum* usher summer in, and the white September trumpets of *L. philippinense formosanum* depart with it. Some lilies have been growing at Winterthur a very long time—among the shrubbery near the Museum, for example, are naturalized plants of the tiger lily, *Lilium tigrinum*, and the leopard lily, *L. pardalinum*, which no one remembers planting—and new hybrids are tried every year. The world of horticulture is witnessing a tremendous boom in lily breeding. Each season, new hybrids and hybrid races are announced as being healthier, more beautiful, and much more desirable than anything that has gone before. These hybrid lilies are well worth growing, and a number are indeed novel; but some of the species lilies are perfection in themselves. They cannot be improved, nor can they be replaced by hybrids. Let us say rather that the new creations supplement their parents. As for the claim that the species are less vigorous than the hybrids, this is to some extent true. On the other hand, very few of the hybrids are entirely flawless. Lilies are, on the whole, a demanding group of plants and not nearly so easy to grow as zinnias and marigolds. But there are species, like the Madonna and tiger lilies, which have persisted in gardens for centuries with little care or attention.

The flowers of all lilies fall into three groups: trumpet lilies, typified by the common Easter lily *(L. longiflorum)*; Turk's-cap lilies, in which the segments of the nodding flower are sharply recurved, as exemplified by the old-fashioned tiger lily; and upright chalice or bowl-shaped lilies, such as our native wood lily or the candlestick lilies *(L. umbellatum)*. Each type produces a different effect in the garden: the trumpet lilies, mostly white, are very bold and commanding; the Turk's-cap lilies possess much delicacy and grace; and the bowl-shaped lilies, which are mostly orange and red, produce great masses of bright color. In the new hybrids, breeders have succeeded in crossing trumpets with Turk's-caps and Turk's-cap with chalice lilies, producing some interesting intermediate types.

Perhaps most widely advertised of the new hybrids is the group known as the "Mid-Century hybrids" because they were produced around 1950. These are hybrids of *L. tigrinum*, a Turk's-cap, and of a bowl-shaped lily of the *L. umbellatum* type. Most of them inherit the stocky growth of the candlestick lily, the great vigor of both parents, and some of the grace of the tiger lily as well. Their colors include yellows, oranges, and reds, and they bloom in late June and July. Their several flowers per stem are slightly reflexed and intermediate in shape and carriage between Turk's-cap and bowl-shape. Because they face outward, rather than upward, they display themselves to great advantage. Easily the most spectacular of this group is the patented clone 'Enchantment,' a vivid nasturtium red. Like the tiger lily, this hybrid bears bulbils in the axils of its leaves which permit easy and quick multiplication without disturbing the original plants. Other good Mid-Century hybrids are the dark red 'Cinnabar,' the bright yellow 'Destiny,' the bright red 'Paprika,' the mahogany-red 'Tabasco,' and the orange 'Valencia.' 'Prosperity,' a fine yellow that

Aurelian Hybrid Lilies

Hanson's Lily. *Lilium Hansoni*

has been highly praised nationally, has proved to be extremely prone to disease at Winterthur. Similar in coloration to the Mid-Century clones is 'Golden Chalice,' a hybrid of the chalice type with warm golden apricot flowers. Beginning in early June, it is one of the first lilies to bloom. Of Turk's-cap form in yellow, orange, and red are the "Fiesta hybrids." The flowers of this graceful group, heavily speckled with black or maroon, appear in July.

Blooming in midsummer is a group of hybrid lilies derived from the yellow Turk's-cap *L. Henryi* and from white trumpets such as *L. Sargentiae* and *L. centifolium* (correctly *L. leucanthemum* var. *chloraster*). These are intermediate between the parents in shape, being large, with long, partially recurved segments. Some are pale yellow and others are white with a wash of warm fawn or buff in the center of the flower. In advanced generation seedlings, yellow Turk's-caps and white trumpets reappear, and occasionally a fine, big yellow trumpet crops up. This group of lilies is known by several names, but the oldest and probably the correct name is *L. × aurelianense* or "Aurelian hybrids." All the Aurelians are tall and showy, and valuable for July and August color.

Finally, there are the showy trumpet hybrids, variously known as 'Centifolium,' 'Shelbourne,' and 'Olympic' hybrids. In color these range from pure white to green or fuchsia. The 'Black Dragon' strain has trumpets which are pure white inside and deep maroon outside. 'Emerald' and 'Green Dragon' strains have trumpets which vary from cool green to chartreuse. And the 'Pink Perfection' strain has trumpets of a deep fuchsine pink, rather a harsh color in combination with yellows and reds, but effective with the greens and whites of the other trumpet lilies.

Species lilies in the area of the Sycamore include the tiny coral lily, *L. pumilum*, which

Lilium cv. 'Tabasco'

Oyama Magnolia.
M. Sieboldii

opens its waxy red Turk's-cap flowers in conjunction with the yellow *L. amabile luteum* in June. Later in the month the chaste white martagon lily, *L. Martagon album,* blooms among late-flowering shrubs. And near the end of June one of the most dependable lily species appears, the Japanese *L. Hansoni.* Closely related to the European martagon lily (and with that species, the parent of a hybrid race of great beauty called "Backhouse hybrids"), the Hanson lily has Turk's-cap flowers with unusually thick, waxy segments of soft fawn orange with a few maroon spots. It is shown (p. 119) against a field of ripe wheat beneath a shimmering blue summer sky.

Few flowers are more highly regarded than magnolias. Our southern species, *Magnolia grandiflora,* is considered by many to be the finest flowering tree in the world, but it is too tender to thrive north of Zone 7. The northern gardener must content himself with other species, such as the star magnolia and the saucer magnolia, both deciduous and both oriental in origin. Also deciduous and oriental in origin, but blooming in summer rather than spring, is the oyama magnolia, *M. Sieboldii,* a magnolia of extraordinary grace and refinement. It becomes in time a tree thirty feet high, but it blooms at an early age, and can, for garden purposes, be considered a large shrub. Its leaves are seldom over six inches long, and its cup-shaped, nodding flowers, borne in June and July, are three or four inches across. Delicately fragrant, they are white, with an unusual ring of bright crimson stamens in the center. Less hardy than some oriental magnolias, this species does well through Zone 6 and further south. Where it can be grown, it should be, for it is one

Candleflower. *Eremurus*

Late Lilac.
Syringa villosa

of Japan's most exquisite gifts to gardens. Because of its restrained growth, it is as well suited to small gardens as to large.

Good companions for late-blooming shrubs are certain liliaceous plants with fanciful common names such as "king's spear," "giant asphodel," "candleflower," "desert candle," and "foxtail-lily," which bear even more fanciful spikes of white, yellow, or pink flowers, sometimes nine feet tall and containing hundreds of flowers per stalk. These are members of the genus *Eremurus*, natives to the cold steppes of Turkestan and to the foothills of the Himalayas. Certain species have long been known in gardens of Europe and America, but many are difficult to cultivate away from their arid homes. Recently, however, several hybrids have appeared that possess enough vigor to make them worthy garden subjects almost anywhere. These usually grow four to six feet tall, are extremely showy, and perhaps look best as bold accents among shrubbery.

Since eremuri are native to dry regions, a well drained soil is necessary in cultivation. And before planting, the soil should be well fertilized, for these plants are gross feeders. In autumn, each dormant root, which rather resembles a small octopus, should be planted at least six inches deep, with the "legs" gently spread so that they radiate outward. These fleshy roots are quite brittle, and must be handled with care. Once established, eremuri need little care beyond a yearly top-dressing with well rotted manure or compost. Since they sprout very early in the spring, a mound of ashes, sand, or other porous material over the crowns insures against frost damage. The broad, grasslike foliage of these plants is in itself attractive, and the tall spikes of flowers in late June and July are spectacular. Most eremuri are hardy through Zone 6, and, with winter protection, probably further north. *Eremurus* is Greek for "solitary tail," an allusion to the flower spike.

For most of us, "lilac" immediately evokes the soft color and sweet smell of the common lilac of early spring. This familiar shrub of the genus *Syringa* belongs in every garden, even though in the eastern United States it is subject in summer to a powdery mildew which disfigures its leaves. Some other lilacs are resistant to mildew, but none, alas, have the fragrance of the old-fashioned lilac.

The genus *Syringa* is divided into two sections: *Vulgares,* of which the common lilac, *Syringa vulgaris*, is the type, and *Villosae,* of which the late lilac, *S. villosa*, is the type. The *Villosae* lilacs bloom a good month later than the common lilac, and are never bothered by powdery mildew. These shrubs have a bushy, rounded habit of growth, and their handsome, quilted, deep green leaves are oval or oblong in shape, quite unlike the heart-shaped leaves of *S. vulgaris*. The attractive June flowers of these lilacs are valuable for their late blooming date. Their fragrance is neither very strong nor very pleasant, resembling that of their close relative, privet.

Syringa villosa, with pale mauve-pink blossoms, is among the best of the group. Equally good are the drooping pink *S. reflexa*, and the old hybrid *S. × Henryi*, a vigorous plant with rich mauve blossoms. Of the several newer hybrids in this group, perhaps the most outstanding are those of *S. villosa × reflexa*, produced in Canada by Isabella Preston. The Preston hybrids (most of which bear the names of Shakespearean heroines), vary in color from near white, through several shades of pink, to mauve. All are excellent for late bloom in the garden.

Two other lilacs, so distinct that some botanists group them in a separate genus, are *S. pekinensis* and *S. amurensis japonica,* both of which grow at Winterthur along with the *Villosae* lilacs and other late shrubs. Whatever their classification, the Peking lilac and the Japanese tree lilac are fine garden plants, bearing in the middle of June immense clusters of small, creamy, privet-like flowers. The habit of both is treelike rather than shrubby, especially the Japanese species, which becomes a small, round-headed tree, rather like an apple or pear. Its bark is unlike that of the conventional lilacs. It is black and glossy like that of a cherry, and is of considerable interest in winter. These lilacs all respond to the same treatment given the common species. *S. amurensis japonica* is hardy to Zone 4, and the *Villosae* lilacs to Zone 2.

No plant is more distinctively American than our own mountain-laurel, *Kalmia latifolia*. The genus *Kalmia*, named after Peter Kalm (1716–79), a Swedish naturalist and associate of Linnaeus who spent three years collecting in North America, contains six species, five native to North America and the sixth native to Cuba. Fortunately for us, *K. latifolia* is not only the most beautiful but the commonest plant in the genus. In Europe it is regarded as a great treasure, but in its native land it is not planted as often as it deserves to be. In flower and in leaf it is fully as ornamental as its close relatives, the widely planted rhododendrons, yet rare indeed is the lawn or shrub border which it graces.

At Winterthur, mountain-laurel is appreciated. In Chandler Woods, a native stand turns a whole hillside pink in late May and early June, and its color is repeated in the flowers of *Primula japonica* in an adjacent swamp. A great drift of it also blooms with the summer shrubs near the Sycamore, its flowers of different shades of pink harmonizing beautifully with the dusky pinks and mauves of the late lilacs nearby. Considerable color variation appears in the flowers of the mountain-laurel, some clones being nearly pure white, and others deep, bright pink. Out of flower, its glossy, evergreen leaves and its pleasing habit are decidedly ornamental. In the wild, it grows from coastal Canada to Florida, and should be hardy throughout Zone 4 and southward. It requires an acid soil

Mountain-Laurel.
Kalmia latifolia

and a fair amount of moisture in summer, as do rhododendrons; any gardener who succeeds with these can grow mountain-laurel to perfection. Though happy in woodland plantings, it blooms more thickly in sun. It is important to start with good plants of this species. If dug from the wild (which in many states is against the law), young plants should be selected. Older plants should be cut back severely after digging, and given a year or two to reestablish themselves. Many nurseries specializing in native plants offer such reestablished specimens at a reasonable price.

Mountain-laurel belongs to the heath family, *Ericaceae*. Actually, it is not a laurel at all; the true laurel *(Laurus nobilis)* of Europe is an entirely unrelated plant. No doubt this species was named laurel by early settlers because its glossy green leaves reminded them of the European plant.

The fragrant snowbell, *Styrax Obassia,* was introduced in 1897, but as yet is seen only in rare plant nurseries and a few gardens in this country. Native to Japan, it is a slow growing tree, ultimately twenty-five feet or so in height, with luxuriant foliage and bold branching. Because the branches, especially on young trees, are quite fastigiate, the habit of the tree is distinctly upright, almost formally so. But excessive formality is dispelled by the lines of the branches themselves, which twist and turn in a pleasing manner. The old bark, light fawn brown in color, tends to shred and fall away from trunk and branches, a feature which, along with the clusters of hard, brown, acorn-like fruits, gives it considerable interest in late autumn and winter.

Fragrant Snowbell. *Styrax Obassia*

The leaves of *Styrax Obassia*, grayish green and rough to the touch, are nearly round in shape and quite large—up to eight inches in diameter. They are decorated at the tips with one or more long, pointed teeth. And the flowers, which come in June, are borne in eight-inch racemes which droop gracefully among the still developing leaves, each single flower a fragrant bell of immaculate white.

Another snowbell, *Styrax japonica*, is probably the commonest of the genus in American gardens. It is a small, round-headed, twiggy tree with small leaves and roundish clusters of white flowers hanging from its horizontal branches—entirely different from *S. Obassia*, which is much more lush and exotic in appearance, and which blooms later in June. Both are worthy plants even for the small garden. They never become too large, and are beautiful without being overpowering. Both species are hardy in Zone 4 and southward. They belong to the *Styracaceae*, "styrax" being the old Greek name for a European species. About a hundred styraxes are known, three of which are native in the southeastern United States. Many of these species yield a gum resin called benzoin which is used in medicine and perfumery.

Along a path leading from the Sycamore to Oak Hill are a number of summer-flowering

Oak-Leaf Hydrangea. *H. quercifolia*

plants. The woodland at the right is planted with such native summer-blooming shrubs as the sweet-pepper bush *(Clethra alnifolia)*, the sweet azalea *(Rhododendron arborescens)*, and the oak-leaf hydrangea *(Hydrangea quercifolia)*. Here is a hydrangea very different from the familiar blue hortensia. One might never identify it as a hydrangea by its leaves alone, for these are large, deep green, and lobed very much like the leaves of the red oak. But the flowers betray its consanguinity with the rest of the hydrangea clan. They appear in elongated clusters, pure white in color, and somewhat resemble the flowers of *H. paniculata* (see page 162). In June, after the blooming season is over, they turn bronze purple and remain this way for much of the summer. In the autumn, the foliage becomes a bright bronzy orange. *H. quercifolia* is hardy from the southern portion of Zone 5 southward. It is native to the woodlands of the southeastern United States, from Kentucky to Alabama and Florida. In cultivation it does best in acid soil and partly shaded situations.

On the slope above the Quarry, dappled in summer by the shade of giant oaks and tulip-trees, grow many fine plants. Here are the tiny hardy cyclamen, *C. europeum* and *C. neapolitanum*, lovely in leaf and flower in summer and fall. Here also grows a race of truly magnificent azaleas which is relatively new in American gardens, the Satsuki azaleas from Japan (sometimes called "Chugai Azaleas" in nursery catalogues). The name means

Satsuki Azalea

"May" in Japanese, for in mild Japan, where the Kurume azaleas flower in April, the late-blooming Satsukis flower in May. In the United States they flower in June, the very last of the evergreen azaleas to bring color to our gardens. Derivatives of *Rhododendron indicum* and its dwarf coastal form *eriocarpum*, these azaleas are low and dense in habit, with glossy leaves and immense flowers. They begin blooming around the first of June in Delaware, and, unlike the Kurumes, open their flowers slowly, over a period of two or three weeks. Though these plants seldom seem smothered by blooms as do the Kurume azaleas, their large flowers give them a certain showiness. One of the finest is the cultivar 'Howraku,' with four-inch flowers that may be pure white, white with a rose blotch or stripes, or solid rose pink. Other clones with large flowers are 'Tama-Sugata,' white with a margin of orange salmon, 'Shikun-Ow,' rich glowing purple with a deeper blotch, and 'Kow-Koku,' which has ruffled and frilled flowers of white with pink variegations. Three very dwarf clones are the white 'Gumpo,' the pink and white 'Gunbi,' and the salmon 'Bunkwa.'

Many other fine cultivars appear in this group and all extend the azalea season considerably. One interesting characteristic is their habit of throwing variegated flowers; it is not unusual to see four or five different colors or patterns on a single plant. As young plants, the Satsuki azaleas are somewhat tender. However, once their stems reach the thickness of a lead pencil they become considerably more hardy, and mature plants are nearly as hardy as the Kurumes.

On the slope near the Satsukis grow three unusual species of large-leaved rhododendron. One of these, *R. brachycarpum*, is almost unique among rhododendrons in being difficult to move as a large plant. The species (hardy to about Zone 4) is a native of Japan, and is rather remotely related to our American *R. catawbiense*. It bears tight trusses of rose flowers

Rose Mallow. *Hibiscus palustris*

in June. Closely related to it is a real rarity, *R. niko-montanum*, from the mountains of Nikko in Japan. As a foliage plant, the Nikko-Mountain rhododendron is outstanding, with large, shining, deep green, convex leaves reminiscent of a giant *Ilex crenata* cv. 'Convexa.' In flower it is also attractive with small, frilled flowers in dense clusters, each individual bloom pure white with a golden blotch. It appears to be as hardy as *R. brachycarpum*. Experts still disagree as to whether it is a distinct species or merely a variety of the yellow-flowered *R. chrysanthum*. The plants at Winterthur came from the seedling beds of the great grower and hybridizer of rhododendrons, Joseph Gable of Stewartstown, Pennsylvania, who grew them from seed received under the name *R. chrysanthum*.

The third species of rhododendron growing here is perhaps the most beautiful—the mandarin rhododendron, *R. discolor*, a native of China, and a member of the illustrious *Fortunei* clan. Treelike in growth, often with a single trunk, and with long narrow leaves, light green above and blue white underneath, *R. discolor* bears in June clusters of huge, long-tubed, flaring flowers of pale pink or white. One thinks of lilies rather than rhododendrons when seeing it for the first time. It is fully hardy in Zone 6 and has succeeded in parts of Zone 5. Being a woodland species in the wild, in cultivation it prefers partial shade and some protection from strong winds. A well grown plant, or rather tree, of *R. discolor* is one of the most splendid sights a garden can offer.

The stream flowing from the Quarry is slowed by several small dams, creating ponds that give pleasure to kingfishers, geese, and mallard ducks, as well as to people. It also provides a site for certain summer-flowering plants which grow best when constantly supplied with an abundance of water. Two of the best of these semi-aquatics are swamp

Rose Mallows. *Hibiscus palustris*

or rose mallow *(Hibiscus)*, and the Japanese iris *(Iris Kaempferi)*. At least three species of rose mallow grow wild in swamps and marshes of eastern North America where they make a spectacle in midsummer with their great cups of pink or white. In the wild forms native to the Northeast, the flowers are either pure white, white with a crimson "eye" or center, pale pink, or deep pink. Some fifty years ago, plantsmen recognized the value of these plants for summer color, and when it was found that they would grow in ordinary garden soil, began to hybridize them. The hardy species were crossed with the somewhat tender *Hibiscus coccineus* from the Gulf states, a tall species with leaves finely dissected like those of a Japanese maple, and huge flowers of tomato red. The resulting hybrids, marketed under such names as "Mallow Marvels," are vigorous, hardy plants with flowers in shades of red as well as pink and white.

The hybrid and species rose mallows grow to a height of five feet or so (taller in wet soil), and bloom through most of summer. They are herbaceous in habit, but so dominant that they give an almost shrubby effect in the landscape. All will grow even in fairly dry soil, but they do best with ample moisture. Showy as the man-made hybrids are, the wild rose mallow, with its crimson-eyed white flowers, is difficult to surpass for cool beauty with just the right touch of color.

Hibiscus is a member of the mallow family, *Malvaceae*. Most of the members of the genus are tropical shrubs much admired for their vivid flowers. Those of *H. Rosa-sinensis* are the blossoms which South Sea maidens wear in their hair. *Hibiscus* is an ancient name, probably derived from ibis, the long-billed wading bird held sacred by the Egyptians, though the exact reference is unclear. One theory is that the sacred ibis fed on this plant, but it seems more likely that the name derives from the fact that the seedpods of many species are long, pointed, and curved, like the bill of the ibis.

Iris Kaempferi, named, as is the torch azalea, for the intrepid Engelbert Kaempfer, is one of the latest of the genus *Iris* to bloom, sending up its faultless flowers above sword-shaped leaves all through late June and early July. The species itself is native to Japan, and is seldom grown in this country. The Japanese irises of gardens are hybrids, some of which have been cultivated for centuries in Japan. In color these hybrids range through shades of blue, violet, rich purple, pinkish mauve, and white. Some are attractively veined and variegated with other shades, and nearly all have a golden streak, called a "signal patch," down the center of their drooping petals. Two types of Japanese irises are cultivated: the single, and the so-called double. Single clones, like those of the wild plant, have three large drooping segments called "falls," and three smaller upright segments called "standards." In the double clones, the standards are as large as the falls, and also droop, giving the effect of a large, six-petaled, saucer-shaped flower. The latter type is much showier, but for purity of form the single type excels. The plant illustrated is a single white, beautiful even in bud.

Japanese irises grow well in ordinary gardens if watered thoroughly during the growing season. Unlike their relatives, the American blue flag *(I. versicolor)* and the yellow water flag of Europe, they are not truly aquatic. These will actually grow in water, and both are abundant in the tidal streams of Delaware. But *I. Kaempferi* likes much water in summer and dry feet in winter. Thus it does best at the edge of a stream or pond rather than in it. It is reputed to be intolerant of lime, but this presents no problem in the acid soils of the East Coast. Farther west, in areas of strongly alkaline soil, it would probably need a bed of especially prepared acid, peaty soil.

A large and highly developed family of world-wide distribution is the iris family, *Iridaceae*. Evolved from lily-like ancestors, irises are unique in possessing three stamens instead of six as do the related lilies and amaryllises. Included in the family are such apparently diverse plants as gladiolus, freesia, and crocus, but by far the most popular of

Japanese Iris. *I. Kaempferi*

all is the genus which gives its name to the family—*Iris*. Together with roses, peonies, and lilies, they are among the most beloved and beautiful plants in our gardens. The history of their cultivation is lost in antiquity. Since ancient times, the white *Iris florentina* has been cultivated for the product obtained from its rhizomes—orris-root, an important ingredient of certain cosmetics, perfumes, and medicines. Another white-flowered species—or as botanists now believe, an extremely ancient hybrid—*I. albicans,* is used by Mohammedans to mark their graves, and with the spread of Islam has become established far beyond its natural range. The well-known *fleur-de-lis* design was taken from an iris, possibly the yellow water flag, *I. Pseudacorus*. This design was important in the Near East as well as in the complex symbolism of medieval heraldry, and is still popular.

Best known of garden irises today are the hybrid descendants of "flags" which are called "tall bearded" irises. Modern breeders have doubled the chromosomes of this group, greatly increasing their stature, size of flower, and vigor. In addition, the substance and texture of the blossoms have been improved, and the range of color greatly expanded. Today's tall bearded irises are giants, three or four feet in height with immense and spectacular flowers in every color except true spectrum red. So spectacular are they that they brook no competition, and thus are extremely difficult to use in the landscape. If one must grow them (and one should, because nothing else is quite like them), an area of the garden should be devoted to them alone. In beds surrounded by lawn and backed by shrubbery, they are superb in early June.

Also growing at Winterthur are quantities of dwarf and "median" bearded irises. These, being beautiful but much less emphatic than the taller types, harmonize with but do not dominate their companions. They are smaller of flower, shorter of stem, spread less rapidly than the tall bearded plants, and require much less care. Some people fail with tall bearded irises because they think of them as poor-soil plants, when actually they are gross feeders. Even poor soil, however, suits the shorter plants. The shorter bearded irises vary from three inches to nearly two feet in height, and they vary in season of bloom from early April to late May. Some also give a bonus crop of flowers in late summer and autumn. One of the best reblooming irises is an old cultivar called 'Autumn Queen,' which produces cool, blue-white flowers on eighteen-inch stems in May and, almost invariably, again in late August and September, when they are the more beautiful for their rarity.

Iris cristata, the crested iris native to America, is a dwarf species inhabiting wooded mountain slopes in the Appalachians. It bears large lavender or white flowers in early spring, the falls of which carry, instead of beards, tiny crestlike or comblike projections. It is one of the few irises that does well under woodland conditions. Similar but larger is the roof iris, *I. tectorum,* of Japan. A charming though perhaps apocryphal tale is associated with this species. It seems that the first western visitors to Japan were surprised to see irises growing in the thatched roofs of buildings. The reason for this, they learned, was that the Emperor of Japan owned every square foot of ground in that country, and decreed just which plants could be grown in it. *Iris tectorum* was not one of these, a fact which distressed the Japanese ladies, for they whitened their faces with a powder made from the ground rhizomes of the plant. But with feminine ingenuity they solved their problem by removing the plants from the Emperor's soil and growing them in the thatch of their housetops.

Clenny Run's busy trip through Winterthur is interrupted at several points by dams which produce ponds of many uses. These still, freshwater ponds help to prevent the loss of topsoil in the form of silt carried by swift-running streams, and they allow part of the fresh water lost daily to seep back into the ground. In addition, they provide feeding, drinking, and resting areas for wild birds and animals.

The margins of a pond create many exciting planting possibilities. Drifts of daffodils

Dwarf Bearded Iris

Rose Planting on Pavilion Drive

are delightful next to an expanse of still water. Trees and shrubs—especially graceful trees like willows—are exceptionally attractive when reflected on the dark surface of a pond. And then, of course, there are the aquatics—waterlilies, certain irises, mallows—which require water, or at least the water's edge, in which to grow. Bridges again give new opportunities for planting. The simple stone bridge across Clenny Run is a case in point. Here the structure itself forms both backdrop and support for red climbing roses, as well as a backdrop for other roses and, in late summer, for the Indian-cup (page 157).

Most roses have a magnificent individuality which does not lend itself to naturalistic planting; thus their use in a landscape is extremely limited. They are usually best suited to rose gardens, particularly the newer hybrid roses, the hybrid teas, floribundas, grandifloras, and climbers. Climbers may be used in semi-naturalistic settings if they have a structure, such as a wall, on which to grow. But for really naturalistic plantings, only the species roses, and just a few of the older hybrid roses, are suitable. The wild roses of the world—*Rosa virginiana, R. setigera, R. Moyesii, R. rugosa, R. spinosissima*—possess natural simplicity as well as great beauty, and can be blended into semi-wild surroundings,

Rosa cv. 'Coral Creeper'

while their fancier (and, it should be added, more disease-prone and troublesome) hybrid relatives are not.

A few hybrids, however, have been bred not so much for classic form of flower as for hardiness, floriferousness, and special uses in the garden. Such are the hybrids 'Coral Creeper' and 'Apricot Glow,' which have single or semi-double flowers, glossy, disease-free foliage, and a trailing rather than upright or climbing habit. Extremely hardy, they are perhaps most valuable as ground cover plants for steep banks and for out-of-the-way spots in the garden where mowing is difficult or undesired. Each plant spreads horizontally, with heavy branches growing parallel to the ground, until it forms an extensive and free-blooming mat of shiny leaves and bright blossoms. The main blooming season is in June, with only occasional flowers during the summer, but the large orange-red hips are showy in the fall. 'Coral Creeper' has single or partially double flowers with all the grace of a wild rose, a soft but bright rose pink. 'Apricot Glow' has semi-double flowers of a soft salmon pink.

The word primrose comes from the Old French *primerole,* which in turn evolved from the Latin *primula,* a diminutive of the word *primus,* "first." In Europe, wild primroses are among the first wildflowers to bloom, and their cultivated progeny grace our early spring gardens here also. But the genus contains numerous species in addition to the three or four wild plants of Europe, many of which are quite different from the bright spring-flowering species.

The genus *Primula,* including over three hundred species, is centered in China. In nature, primulas are herbaceous plants native to woodlands, bogs, and alpine screes and

Hybrid Candelabra
Primula

moraines. The one thing that all these areas have in common is an abundance of readily available moisture at root level. Those that are woodland plants—the European species are good examples—are best adapted to garden culture, since few yards have either bogs or melting glaciers. Thus the woodland primulas, which bloom and make their best growth early in the year before the trees leaf out and shade them too heavily, are the best known of the genus. The alpine species are the most difficult to grow and the least known. Like many alpine plants, they are diminutive, and while exquisite, are not showy. They require summers so cool that their culture is difficult in most of the United States. The bog primulas are somewhere in between the other two types as far as difficulty of cultivation is concerned. Their one demand—much water in summer—can be met with a little attention, and if they are grown in partial shade they often succeed quite well in the ordinary garden. In the bog garden, however, they are at their best, and their best is truly superb. The grounds at Winterthur are blessed with several boggy areas, and full advantage is taken of the opportunity to use these unusual plants.

Like the woodland primroses, in spring these plants send up rosettes of oval or strap-shaped leaves from a central point called the "crown." And, like the woodland plants, they later send up a scape—an unbranched, leafless stalk bearing a head of flowers at its apex—from the center of this crown. But here the resemblance ends. For the apex of most bog primulas continues to grow after it produces its first head of flowers. It elongates a few inches, another cluster of flowers arises, and it elongates again. Since these scapes

Candelabra Primula on Stream below Pavilion Drive. *P. japonica*

commonly grow two or three feet tall, with several whorls of flowers spaced at intervals along their upper portions, their total effect is showy in the extreme, yet quite graceful and charming. An added bonus is a very long season of bloom. Because of their whorled flowers, these plants are often called "candelabra primulas."

It is horticultural convention to call only the early-flowering English species "primrose," and to call the rest of the genus "primulas." The candelabra primulas are chiefly native to Asia, centered in the Himalayas and western China. Several species span nearly the whole color range of the genus—yellow, orange, red, purple, white, and pink. One of the best is an outlying species from Japan, *Primula japonica*. A fairly foolproof rule of horticulture is that plants native to Japan are well adapted to the climate of eastern North America, while plants from China are not. This certainly applies to *P. japonica;* it is the easiest of the candelabra primulas for gardens in the eastern United States. The Chinese and Himalayan candelabras can be grown here, but they are much less flexible in their needs, and really do best in a bog or along the edge of a pond. *P. japonica* will usually succeed in moisture-retentive garden soil if it is not allowed to suffer too much from summer drought.

The crown of *P. japonica* may reach the size of a man's fist, and its rosette of light green, toothed leaves resembles a head of lettuce. The color of its flowers is bright wine red with a tiny yellow, or sometimes a darker red eye. It has several color variants in pink, rose, white, and red. 'Millar's Crimson' is one of the best of these, a vivid carmine in color, but all the variants are attractive and harmonize well with each other. At Winterthur the species has grown in an old quarry for decades; more recently, a multitude of seedlings has been planted along the wet, springy banks of a small stream. Here they begin blooming in May in every shade from white to deep crimson, and last well into June, providing a streak of rich color across the green lawn of early summer.

In the Quarry at Winterthur grow many kinds of primulas. Here *Primula japonica* is strictly banned, being too vigorous and aggressive; in its place grow the more difficult Chinese and Himalayan species. A few of these have failed, but many have succeeded admirably—for example the two pale yellow species *P. helodoxa* and *P. prolifera*. These are almost identical: tall and slender, willowy in effect, with many whorls of canary yellow flowers borne on scapes covered with a silvery, mealy substance. *P. helodoxa*, whose specific name in Greek means "glory of the marsh," is the more vigorous, second only to *P. japonica* in ease of culture in American gardens. It blooms in late May and June, and blooming with it is the pale mauve *P. Beesiana*, giving a pleasing echo of the mauve-yellow combinations seen earlier in spring. Also in late May appear the orange-yellow *P. Bulleyana* and the burgundy *P. pulverulenta*. The last named is another easily grown species. Its rich flowers may approach magenta too closely to suit the taste of some, but they are nevertheless handsomely set off by the thick layer of silvery dust (known technically as *farina)* which coats the buds and stems. A very beautiful soft pink variant of this species is known in the trade as "Bartley Strain." Among the more difficult primulas in the Quarry are *P. aurantiaca*, an orange species that is attractive but none too permanent, and *P. Cockburniana*. A brilliant, eye-searing cinnabar orange, the latter is the brightest of all, but alas the most fickle. It usually blooms once in a blaze of glory, and fails to return the following year.

P. Cockburniana and several other species figure in the parentage of the new hybrid primulas now available. These are stunning plants in shades of orange, apricot, pink, scarlet, crimson, mauve, and purple, and all are blessed with a hybrid vigor which makes them comparatively easy to grow. Perhaps the best known of these are the Asthore hybrids and the Inshriach hybrids, both of which originated in the British Isles.

The path that leads from the Pavilion to both gardens and Museum is interesting throughout the year. Running along it is a fern garden planted with nearly every species

Hybrid Candelabra Primulas in Quarry

Fern Planting and Rosebay Rhododendron. *R. maximum*

of native fern that will grow in this area, and a few hardy exotic ferns as well. This shady little nook is always a delight, for though ferns have no flowers, they are fresh looking and attractive, and the various species differ so much in appearance that a mixed planting of them is never dull. The tall, plumy ostrich fern and the robust cinnamon fern and giant woodfern give height and accent to beds of glossy green Christmas fern, pale, delicate New York fern, and gray-green silvery spleenwort. Also growing here are the beech and oak ferns, the many different woodferns of the genus *Dryopteris,* the chain fern, the sensitive fern, and the lady fern. The names of the two latter ferns—in both English and Latin— are somewhat misleading. There is nothing sensitive in the appearance of the sensitive fern, *Onoclea sensibilis;* on the contrary, it is one of the coarsest and most vigorous of all ferns. But it is so sensitive to cold that its fronds are reputed to wither at the merest hint of frost. The lady fern, *Athyrium Filix-femina,* is a delicately cut, lacy thing, though there is nothing ladylike in the vigor with which it grows. But the story goes that Linnaeus, who named the plant, was so exasperated with its extreme variability (there are literally dozens of forms and varieties of the species) that he named it in allusion to a phrase from Virgil, *Varium et mutabile semper femina,* probably best translated by Tennyson's "Woman is various and most mutable."

Some of the ferns in the fern garden at Winterthur are delicate species that grow in the wild clefts and crevices of rock, and are quite difficult to please under cultivation. A rock substitute has been found for them in the rim of the retaining wall beside the path. Here grow mats of the dwarf, evergreen common polypody, the tiny woodsias, the exceedingly delicate maindenhair spleenwort, and even a plant or two of the odd walking fern,

Rosebay Rhododendron. *R. maximum*

which forms tiny new plants at the tip of each frond, and in the wild grows only in north-facing crevices of limestone rocks.

American greenhouses abound with tender exotic ferns, but exotic ferns suitable for outdoor culture are rare in this country. Two that are distinct enough to warrant growing are the Japanese or red-fruited woodfern *(Dryopteris erythrosora),* and the Japanese painted spleenwort *(Athryium Goeringianum pictum).* The Japanese woodfern grows about two feet tall, and its dark, glossy fronds are evergreen. The young fronds as they unroll change from mahogany to bronze, and finally to a deep, polished green, with bright red fruit-dots on the old fronds. It is extremely beautiful, and as showy as many flowering plants. Judging from its performance at Winterthur, it should be hardy through Zone 6. Worth noting is the fact that its lacy fronds hold up well when cut (many ferns wilt immediately), a virtue which might endear it to florists were it more widely known.

It is hard to conceive of a fern deserving the epithet "gaudy," yet the painted spleenwort almost merits it. Its mature fronds are light green, variegated with silvery gray and pale pink. Seldom growing more than a foot in height, it is a hardy and easily grown fern, much like the related lady fern in appearance and characteristics (in fact, it is often called "variegated lady fern"). Among plain green ferns or broad-leaved evergreens it makes an elegant accent during the growing season. The fronds die back to the ground in the winter. In Zone 6 it is fully hardy, and since it is deciduous, it will probably thrive further north.

Helping to shade the fernery at Winterthur is an ancient specimen of the rosebay rhododendron, *Rhododendron maximum,* the only large-leaved rhododendron native in the north-eastern United States, and one of the very first in cultivation, having been introduced into England in 1736. Rhododendron specialists, particularly in England and in the Pacific Northwest, treat this plant cavalierly because it is far less flamboyant than the magnificent Asian species so easily grown in those areas. But we in the East cannot afford to sneer at broad-leaved evergreens of any kind, however dull the blossoms. The *R. maximum* may be one of the least spectacular species in flower, but it has virtues often overlooked, the foremost being its late season of bloom. I have seen specimens in Delaware in bloom on the Fourth of July. Another virtue is its color, shell pink fading to white, with none of the muddy purple that so often flaws the hardy *R. catawbiense* and its hybrids. A final virtue is its hardiness and adaptability. Most rhododendrons cannot endure the extremes of heat and cold in the eastern United States—sometimes a yearly range of a hundred degrees. Complicating the difficulties caused by this great range is the fact that zero weather is often accompanied by strong winds, and summer heat by periods of prolonged drought. Small wonder that plants adapted to less extreme climates fail here. But the rosebay rhododendron is adapted to these extremes because it evolved in the Northeast, and it withstands our harsh climate better than any other rhododendron. In nature a large shrub, in protected valleys sometimes a small tree up to forty feet in height, *R. maximum* (named "largest" by Linnaeus because of its stature) is unsuited to foundation planting except around the biggest houses. In the natural surroundings of shady open woodland, however, it is not only one of the most trouble-free but one of the noblest of the rhododendron clan.

The Pool Garden is different in character from the rest of Winterthur. None of the expansive naturalness characteristic of the gardens is found in this neatly contrived little assembly of colorful flowers and pleasing architecture. The architecture of the area is not that of nature but of man; walls, gates, hedges, straight paths, and the long rectangle of the swimming pool bound its vistas. Nowhere can one look and see the horizon. It is a microcosm, completely isolated from the rest of the gardens.

There are three entrances to the Pool Garden: one from the west, down the long flight of steps from the Museum; one from the east, through gates that lead past the bath-houses; and one from the south, through green wooden gates. The first two entrances give

Clematis cv. 'Ramona'

an immediate glimpse of the swimming pool, which dominates the view; the third does not, and is perhaps the most charming. When the wooden gates are closed, a view of the garden is difficult, but when the gates are open, warm, bright color leaps to the eye.

Orange daylilies, wax begonias with burnished leaves almost as colorful as their flowers, spiky snapdragons, chamomile with flowers like little sunbursts, filmy meadow-rue, crystalline blue lobelias, pink foxgloves, and multicolored pansies all bloom in season and wash the garden in the colors of summer.

Near the pool, tropical looking yuccas open creamy bells, Gnarled, ancient plants of lavender, and carpets of lamb's-tongue, both with gray, aromatic foliage, open their flowers in the summer heat. In pots, ornamental jardinieres, and lead tanks, are ivy, variegated *Vinca major*, and *Sedum Sieboldii,* its trailing stems beaded with succulent, orbicular blue leaves. Here the taste for annuals, for bedding plants, for variegated foliage, for plants in ornate containers, in short, for all the interesting plants that do not fit into a naturalistic landscape, can be indulged. It is a summer place, bathed in Mediterranean warmth and color, a garden designed for privacy and relaxation.

Two excellent plants for summer bloom are *Clematis* and *Sorbaria,* as different from each other as two flowers can be, yet each lovely in its own way. *Clematis* is a genus of nearly three hundred species of woody vines or herbaceous perennials native throughout most of the northern hemisphere. The name (pronounced with the accent on the first syllable) is derived from the Greek *klema,* meaning tendril, and alludes to the plant's

False-Spirea.
Sorboria arborea

method of climbing. Clematis flowers may be small and borne abundantly in large clusters, as in the sweet smelling virgin's-bowers, or they may be large, solitary, and showy in the extreme, as in most of the hybrids grown for ornament in occidental gardens.

Illustrated is one of the best of the large-flowered cultivars, the blue-mauve or lilac 'Ramona,' a hybrid of the large-flowered *Clematis lanuginosa*. Many hybrids of this type are commercially available, all distinguished by their large flowers and by the fact that they bloom on new shoots made in spring, and may therefore be pruned sharply in late fall or early spring. Like several other genera of the *Ranunculaceae* (notably *Anemone, Caltha*, and *Helleborus*), *Clematis* has no petals, the showy parts of the flower being sepals that have become petal-like. This peculiarity, however, is of interest mainly to the botanically inclined; to the casual eye the bright sepals are indistinguishable from petals.

Nearly every member of the genus is ornamental. The large-flowered hybrids like 'Ramona' are not the easiest plants to grow, but they are not so difficult as they are reputed to be. All they need is a rich soil which is well drained but not dry, abundant moisture during the summer months, and a ground cover of some sort to keep the soil at their roots from baking. They do especially well among low shrubs. An occasional application of ground limestone is beneficial in areas where the soil is strongly acid, since they prefer a sweet soil. Pruning is difficult to advise, for different sections of the genus require different treatment. 'Ramona' and related hybrids which bloom on new wood may be—indeed should be—pruned in early spring to encourage strong new growth. The rich purple

C. Jackmani and the soft pink *C. montana rubens* should be pruned just after blooming, since these bloom on last year's wood.

Sorbaria is a small genus of the rose family, *Rosaceae*, closely allied to and once included in *Spiraea*. It shows its relationship to the spireas in its clusters of tiny white flowers, but there the resemblance ends. For sorbarias lack the small leaves and restrained growth of spireas. They are tall, vigorous, lush-growing shrubs which often reach the size of small trees, and their abundant, compound leaves resemble those of locust or mountain-ash. The generic name comes from the Latin *Sorbus*, mountain-ash, and alludes to the similarity of leaf in the two plants. Many garden writers have called these plants coarse, but to my mind little about them is coarse. They are unsuited to foundation planting, but as specimen plants for the lawn or in shrub borders they are stunning. Their leaves, while large, have a graceful fernlike quality, and display one of the most vivid deep greens in nature. And they bloom throughout the summer, when blooming shrubs are scarce.

The huge panicles of flowers are attractive enough on the plant, but when cut and brought indoors they become much more beautiful. One panicle makes a bouquet, and at close range the individual white flowers, each five-petaled with a large puff of wiry white filaments, are as light and airy as a spring day. There are about eight species in the genus. *Sorbaria arborea*, illustrated on p. 145, and the similar but lower-growing *S. Aitchisoni* are hardy from Zone 6 southward. Also similar is *S. sorbifolia*, the hardiest of the genus, which thrives from Zone 2 southward.

Oak Hill is named, of course, for its oak trees. At Winterthur, only three species of oak—red, black, and white—are common in the wild, but on Oak Hill several other species are established. Here is the pin oak *(Quercus palustris)*, with its finely cut leaves and characteristically drooping branches; the scarlet oak *(Q. coccinea)*, with its unusually flamboyant autumn color; the shingle oak *(Q. imbricaria)*, remarkable for its lance-shaped, most un-oaklike leaves; and the exotic Turkey oak *(Q. cerris)*, whose name refers to the tree's habitat in Asia Minor. This last is one of the best of the oaks, a round-headed, dense-foliaged tree, which may reach one hundred feet in height. Its deep, glossy green leaves are five or so inches in length, with small wavy teeth along their margins. They have no autumn color to speak of, but remain green far into the season, providing an excellent contrast with other deciduous trees. The acorn of the Turkey oak, two inches long, cylindrical in shape, and half-covered by a great, rough, turban-shaped cap is a most attractive feature. Finally, this oak is one of the easiest to transplant, and makes a most desirable shade tree. However, as a native of warm Mediterranean regions, it is not so hardy as the native oaks and will probably not succeed north of Zone 6.

Gardeners tend to avoid oaks because of the prevalent myth that they are slow-growing. Actually they grow as rapidly as most trees once they are established, and are really more desirable than the popular maples because their deep roots do not seriously interfere with the roots of adjacent plants. Their only drawback, in fact, derives from this very virtue, for being deep-rooted, they are more difficult to transplant in large sizes than are shallower-rooted trees.

Oaks form the architecture of Oak Hill. To delight the eye, the area also has plants with conspicuous flowers: mock-oranges, deutzias, late lilacs, azaleas, and spireas, all coming in early June in great waves of mauve, pink, and white. Mock-oranges are old-fashioned plants. For many of us, the clear, sweet scent of "syringas," as they are sometimes called, is blended with memories of childhood days when summer seemed an eternity. The "syringa" of old was *Philadelphus coronarius*, a native of Europe. It has four-petaled white flowers, and came to be called mock-orange because its scent resembles that of true orange flowers. The name syringa is appropriate for this plant, since its stems may well have provided material for the *syrinx* or Pan-pipes played by Greek shepherds, but it is

Hybrid Mock-Orange.
Philadelphus × Lemoinei

unfortunately both botanically untenable and confusing. In spite of the fact that this genus was already known colloquially as syringa, Linnaeus for some reason named it for Ptolemy Philadelphus, king of Egypt in the third century before Christ. To a wholly unrelated genus, the lilacs, he gave the generic name *Syringa*. Thus syringa today means lilac to some and mock-orange to others.

Mock-oranges are members of the woody branch of the saxifrage family. They are very closely related to *Deutzia* and not far removed from *Hydrangea*. *Philadelphus coronarius* is only one of about forty species in the genus, all of which are native in Europe, Asia, and the Americas. In addition, many excellent hybrids have been produced, most of them in the nineteenth century by the French breeder Lemoine. *P. × Lemoinei* is a hybrid group characterized by dwarf stature. One of the finest of the named clones of this group is the low, floriferous 'Avalanche.' Other good hybrids are *P. × virginalis,* and the transcendently beautiful 'Belle Etoile.'

For Americans, the name "dogwood" automatically brings to mind the flowering dogwood, *Cornus florida*, native to the eastern United States. But there are forty-odd species of dogwood in the world, many of which are quite different in appearance from *C. florida*. The bunchberry *(C. canadensis)*, for example, has typical dogwood flowers, but is a tiny undershrub or half-herbaceous plant only about six inches high. It carpets the floors of forests in Canada and the northern United States. The "typical" dogwood flowers of bunchberry and flowering dogwood are actually not typical at all. Such showy inflores-

148

Japanese Dogwood.
Cornus Kousa

cences are relatively rare in the genus. Most dogwoods have clusters of tiny, insignificant flowers like those of their distant relatives, viburnums, elders, and carrots, and are grown for their beauty of leaf, fruit, or brightly colored bark.

The petals of the flowering dogwood are actually not petals but bracts—colored, modified leaves—surrounding the compound head of flowers. Many other plants have showy bracts rather than petals—the florist's poinsettia, for example. In the flowering dogwood the bracts are four, and roughly spoon-shaped. Another dogwood, *C. Kousa* from Japan, has bracted flowers which rival the American species in beauty.

The Japanese dogwood blooms in June, a full month later than the American species, and its bracts are pointed rather than rounded or square at the tips. It is a small, pyramidal tree with exfoliating bark that is attractive in winter, and, since it blooms when its leaves are fully expanded, the total effect in flower differs from that of *C. florida*. The latter species in bloom is a mass of white or pink, but *C. Kousa* consists of hundreds of white stars set in a background of soft green. The fruits of the two species differ also. Each bracted flower cluster of *C. florida* produces in autumn several glossy scarlet berries, whereas each bracted cluster of *C. Kousa* produces a single, large, conglomerate fruit, soft in texture, pinkish red in color, and faintly reminiscent of a strawberry. The Japanese dogwood is not planted nearly as often as it should be. It is one of the few exceptions to the rule that exotic plants are more popular in America than their native counterparts, for, whereas most lawns in America boast at least one American dogwood, the Japanese species is usually seen only in public gardens and arboretums. The Chinese form of the species *(C. Kousa chinensis,* which bears the absurd common name "Chinese Japanese Dogwood")* is somewhat showier than the type because of its larger bracts. This form was introduced into America by E. H. Wilson in 1908. An old and particularly fine specimen of it, possibly from Wilson's original plants, grows at Winterthur at the golf course edge of the Azalea Woods. *Cornus Kousa* is a superb ornamental, hardy in Zone 6 and possibly farther north. It should be grown wherever it will succeed, for it complements, rather than competes with, its American relative.

White—of dogwood, deutzia, mock-orange, and spirea—is the predominant color in early June on Oak Hill. Other colors do occur: pink and mauve in late lilacs; rose, red, and lavender in azaleas; red and salmon pink in buckeyes. And beneath the oaks, wild azaleas bloom in yellow, salmon, pink, white, and flaming orange. But in the main, Oak Hill in June is a sea of white flowers.

Among the first spireas to bloom in late May is *Spiraea cantoniensis* and its hybrid *S.×Vanhouttei*. These are spireas of the bridal wreath type—spreading shrubs with arching branches set at flowering time with tight, round clusters of white flowers—each a tiny nosegay in itself. Similar, but coming considerably later, and therefore valuable for extending the season of bloom, is *S. nipponica,* a handsome plant which should be grown more often than it is. A clone of this species is currently offered by a major nursery under the name 'Snowmound.'

The bridal wreaths are among the earliest of the spireas. All have white flowers, some of which are extremely precocious. *S. Thunbergi,* the earliest of all, opens its fragile white flowers along with the daffodils in April. Blooming toward the middle of June are two different types of spireas, both with pink or, rarely, with white flowers. The hybrid *S.×Margaritae* is typical of one kind; it is a low, spreading shrub with dense branches, each terminating in a broad, flat cluster of dusky, rose-pink blossoms. The old 'Anthony Waterer' is a hybrid of the same group. Similar but much smaller is *S.×Lemoinei alpestris,* which has become widely circulated in the trade under the erroneous name of *Spiraea japonica alpina.* It is a delightful little plant, restrained enough even for rock garden use.

The other type of late-blooming spirea is typified by the meadowsweets and the hardhacks and steeplebushes which grow wild in this country. These are usually vigorous, upright shrubs with cylindrical spikes of dusky rose in summer. Because of their ease of culture and their informal habit, they are excellent for naturalistic plantings. Most of the steeplebush spireas in cultivation are hybrids, the commonest of all being probably *S.×Billiardi.* Similar is *S.×macrothyrsa,* a hybrid growing about four feet in height, with stiff, upright stems rising from a suckering rootstock. It quickly forms a low, dense thicket, surmounted in summer by many long, graceful plumes of rose flowers.

Species in each of the three sections of the genus *Spiraea* cross readily with other species within the same section, but hybrids between members of different sections are produced only with some difficulty. These occasional intersectional hybrids are often extremely showy. A good example is *S.×sanssouciana,* a hybrid between one of the pink steeplebushes and one of the summer-blooming, flat-headed pink species. One of the most floriferous of spireas, it is intermediate between its parents, with fat, conical heads of rose flowers blooming in the middle of June.

Complementing these spireas are many choice summer-blooming plants: yellow hawkweeds, pink and white indigos, rose campions, orange butterflyweed, and a summer-blooming squill *(Scilla chinensis)* with starry rose-pink flowers. Most of these are herbaceous. The pink indigo, *Indigofera Kirilowii,* is a low shrub, very attractive with its pealike blossoms; its white relative, *I. incarnata alba,* is a shrubby plant that dies almost to the ground in the latitude of Delaware. The campion, *Silene Armeria,* is an annual which

Reeve's Spirea.
Spiraea cantoniensis

reseeds itself each year. Showiest of all is the fiery butterflyweed, *Asclepias tuberosa*, a species of milkweed which brightens fields and roadsides throughout much of the United States. It is typically a clear, flamboyant orange, but forms range from near scarlet to canary yellow. In cultivation it is one of the finest garden subjects, thriving in any well drained soil as long as it receives some sun during the day. The plant is perennial and may be started from seeds or transplanted from the wild. Since its roots are large and fleshy, considerable care is required in digging in order to avoid injuring them. In nature it is found from New England south to Florida and west to Minnesota, Colorado, and Arizona. It seems indifferent to soil acidity; it grows with equal abandon in the stony, near-sterile soil of upland pastures, and on the sunny edges of the rich, acid pinewoods of the South.

Among the last of the late-blooming spring shrubs is the elegant and aptly named fringe-tree, *Chionanthus virginicus*. The last week of May sees this large shrub producing hanging clusters of fleecy white flowers. Chionanthus is an extreme example of the ornamental native plant unappreciated on its home grounds. It is widely planted in Europe, where it is considered one of the finest introductions from America, yet here it is almost invariably passed by in favor of exotic plant material. Its merits are many: foremost are its unique flowers, but it also has lovely fruits—grapelike clusters of blue berries—and its leaves turn bright yellow in autumn. It is tolerant of a wide range of soils; it grows quickly, is easy to transplant, and has a pleasing habit and good foliage. On the negative side, it is

American Fringe-Tree.
Chionanthus virginicus

susceptible to the same scale that attacks its relatives the lilacs, and its flowers are often functionally unisexual—that is, some plants bear only female flowers while others bear only male flowers. While the male flowers are larger and showier than the female, they do not unfortunately produce the berries that are so attractive in the fall. All in all, however, it is a most desirable plant. Chionanthus is native in damp woods from Pennsylvania to Florida and west to Missouri, Oklahoma, and Texas, and is hardy from Zone 4 southward. After many years of growth it becomes almost treelike, reaching occasionally a height of thirty-five feet. A Chinese relative, *C.retusus,* is similar, but smaller and more refined in all its parts. It is hardy from Zone 5 (possibly the southern portion of Zone 4) southward.

As the June days lengthen, the garden becomes tranquil with the peace of early summer. Warm, brief showers unfix the last of the azalea flowers from ovaries already swelling with seed. Brown and bedraggled, their season's work done, they fall away and are swallowed up in the quickly growing grass. In odd corners, foxglove beard-tongue *(Penstemon Digitalis)* shows white, and an occasional rogue daylily displays orange flowers. Otherwise each day is a celebration in green. The trees are heavy with foliage; the grass a fresh and fragrant green carpet.

The first of the young birds are out of the nest. Young robins, their spotted breasts betraying their thrush ancestry, follow busy parents about the lawns. Clamoring adolescent crows pursue their parents darkly from tree to tree. Young cardinals pipe sibilantly

Pinetum and Sundial Garden

from the depths of the densest shrubbery. Adult chickadees and nuthatches are much in evidence, searching tree trunks, twigs and branches, but they are silent, diligent, hurried, not at all the friendly and inquisitive birds they were in winter. Their young are seldom seen; perhaps they leave their nests later than most birds. Also unseen in June are the young of the goldfinch, for, like the grasshopper, the goldfinch plays his summer away; not until August will he mold his cup of thistledown and raise his young. And somewhere on the lawn will be sitting that most clamorous of birds, the baby cowbird, all beady eyes and gaping beak, calling ceaselessly, piteously for the food supplied it by its foster parents, a pair of tiny and overworked yellow warblers or song sparrows.

Winterthur abounds with wildlife. Most evident of course is what might be termed the "minor order" of wild creatures—rabbits, squirrels, groundhogs, and the perching birds, from finches and sparrows to crows. Seldom encountered but nonetheless present are the larger and warier animals—game birds, birds of prey, the larger mammals. Some, like the wild geese and ducks, have learned to take advantage of the sanctuary Winterthur offers, and have become tame. Others retain their wariness. Doves coo in the pines all spring and summer, but lapse into silence at the approach of a human being. Cock pheasants crow in the meadows; occasionally they are seen strutting in metallic splendor along the roadsides, or scaling over the Pinetum, but they have wisely learned not to trust man, and vanish at his approach. There are foxes at Winterthur, though one seldom sees the sly, handsome creatures. Deer live in the woodland, but the most one sees are their tracks in the mud of streambanks.

The grounds here are subdued but by no means tamed. Where visitors walk and chat comfortably by day, the life and death drama of the natural world is enacted by night. Little evidence of this nocturnal activity remains after sunrise: perhaps a string of rabbit tracks, a tuft of hair or a few scattered feathers beneath a bush, or the feather and bone leavings of an owl.

The conifers in the Pinetum change little with the seasons. Spring's new growth is a fresher, brighter green than last year's needles. The developing cones of some spruces and pines are rather bright in color, and the male cones of all the conifers produce a snowstorm of yellow pollen when they open in spring. But generally speaking, this group of evergreens is the one most nearly changeless element in the whole garden, providing the needed contrast with the more variable elements, the deciduous flowering plants. Salmon, yellow, and orange Ghent and Mollis azaleas seem the more flamboyant among dark evergreens; white azaleas seem whiter, red azaleas a deeper red. Even tiny plants—daffodils, dogtooth-violets, corydalis—seem brighter in the evergreen shade.

Lilies, especially, are complemented by evergreens, and the trees protect them from wind. Fallen needles provide the summer mulch necessary for their best growth, and the rich, acid accumulation of humus beneath the conifers is an excellent addition to the soil in which they are planted. Lilies will not of course flourish in dense shade directly beneath the trees. They will grow, but they will lean toward the sun and be bowed to the ground by the slightest amount of wind or rain. In sunny glades between the trees, however, they flourish beautifully, and are a welcome bit of summer color.

If summer-flowering shrubs are rare, rarer still are trees that blossom in the heat of summer. And rarest of all are trees that show yellow color in summer. There are in fact only two trees hardy in the North that have bright yellow flowers. One is the spring-blooming *Laburnum*, or golden-chain, and the other is the July-blooming *Koelreuteria paniculata*, the golden-rain tree. Similar as the common names of these two trees are, the plants themselves are totally different. *Laburnum* belongs to the pea family, is native to Europe, and does not care for the hot summers of eastern North America. *Koelreuteria*, a native of the Orient, is a member of the soapberry family *(Sapindaceae)*, and thrives in hot, dry weather. The soapberry family, which includes about one thousand species, is almost wholly tropical. Hardy species are found only in the genera *Xanthoceras, Koelreuteria,* and *Sapindus*. The soapberries are of great economic importance in the tropics: the fruits of some species are edible and those of other kinds yield useful oils. Fruits of the genus *Sapindus* contain an alkaline principle called saponin which cleanses like soap, whence the names soapberry and *Sapindus* (literally "soap of India" in Latin).

Widespread though they are in the tropics, soapberries are not significant in gardens of the temperate zone. Those species which can be grown are, however, quite interesting and beautiful. *Xanthoceras* was mentioned earlier; *Koelreuteria* is commoner in America, especially in the Midwest. The mystical "Golden Raintree" which figured in the novel *Raintree County* was no doubt this species. Actually, I have always thought "golden-rain tree" an inappropriate name. With its upright panicles of yellow blossoms, the tree looks more like a golden fountain than golden rain. The tree is also called, with similar lack of logic, "pride of India" (although it is not native to India), "China tree," and "varnish tree," names which more properly belong to entirely unrelated trees. Whatever it is called, the golden-rain tree is a valuable flowering tree, not only for its time of bloom but for sheer

Golden-Rain Tree. *Koelreuteria paniculata*

beauty. It grows ultimately into a heavy-branched, round-headed tree thirty or forty feet in height, with finely divided foliage. The flowers, which make the tree a sunburst in July, are clear bright yellow, and are followed by golden green, papery, Chinese-lantern fruits which are highly ornamental. It thrives even in poor, dry soil, but it should have full sun. It is hardy in Zone 4, and is a worthy addition to any garden, even the small one, because of its outstanding ornamental qualities.

The charm of the exotic often blinds us to the virtues of domestic goods of all kinds, including plants. Nearly every dooryard in this country possesses at least one forsythia, spirea, weigela, or lilac, all of which hail from the Orient. The mountains of Appalachia are brilliant with myriad native azaleas each year, yet the commonest azaleas in our gardens were originally imported from Japan. Most people are in fact much surprised when they learn that America has wild azaleas. This is not to say that native plants should be given precedence over imports. Indeed, our gardens would be sad places were it not for these exotics. But the natives should not be ignored; there is room for both.

American plants are usually far more appreciated in Europe than at home. Perhaps

Golden-Rain Tree.
Koelreuteria paniculata

this is to be expected, for there they are the exotics. Such plants as the American mountain-laurel, fringe-tree, various native azaleas, and shadbushes are regarded as indispensable shrubs in European gardens, while here they are seldom grown. Time and time again, lovely native vegetation is stripped from woods and fields and replaced by blatant forsythia and one-season bridal wreath.

Nor are native shrubs the only neglected plants. One of America's greatest treasures is its abundance of summer and autumn-blooming wildflowers. The genus *Aster*, for example, comprises over two hundred species, nearly all of which are native to America. Yet the wild asters of America had to go to England as "Michaelmas daisies," there to be improved and hybridized, before we began growing them in our gardens. And that lowly weed goldenrod, ignored by nearly everyone but those who falsely blame it for causing hay fever, is grown and much appreciated as a late-blooming perennial in England. It is worth noting in passing that at least one American nursery has begun to sell goldenrods—not under that name, of course, but under their perhaps more impressive Latin name *Solidago*.

A native plant that gives a wonderfully showy effect in the right setting is the Indian-cup, or cup-plant, *Silphium perfoliatum*. A member of the daisy family, and a close relative of the sunflowers, this plant has thick, four-angled stems which bear, spaced along their length, pairs of large leaves which are perfoliate, or joined at the base, thus forming a cup that actually catches rainwater. In August, great branched clusters of yellow flowers rise

Indian-Cup. *Silphium perfoliatum*

above the handsome leaves, and last well into September. Since the plants grow to six feet or so in height, they are a bit coarse for ordinary situations in the garden, but they are invaluable in places where a great splash of color or a bold accent is needed. Such situations abound at Winterthur.

Another American plant that grows at Winterthur and is considered a great treasure in Europe is the gorgeous cardinalflower. In wet woods, swamps, and the borders of marshes, this gem of a plant raises its tall wands of gleaming, bright red in late August and September. The cardinalflower, botanically *Lobelia cardinalis,* does well in the garden if it is planted in a rich soil and watered copiously during the summer. It is one of the showiest of all plants, native or exotic, and well worth a place in any garden.

One of my finest memories of wildflowers is a sunny glade in the center of a wet wood overgrown with cardinalflowers in full bloom and elderberries heavy with fruit. Everywhere scarlet spikes gleamed among the dense green vegetation of the glade, contrasting sharply in form and color with the elders, which drooped with the weight of their heads of maroon berries. It would have been a barbaric combination of colors anywhere but in those wilds, where nature's harmonizing hand had placed it. The glade was alive with hummingbirds, glittering green and iridescent scarlet, feeding on the nectar of the cardinalflowers. It was morning, and the dew of the night before still sparkled in the soft, slanting rays of the morning sun. The whir of the wings of the fearless, darting little birds was the only sound, loud in the quiet of the summer morning. It was one of nature's great spectacles—color, movement, and the peace found only in truly wild places.

Spring is an extrovert. It leads us from one place to another, choosing its own colors as it goes, silencing any protests we may have with yet another picture postcard scene around the next bend. It sells itself. It is so much drama and spectacle that it does not need substance. But summer hides its light under the proverbial bushel, keeps silent, holds its charms hidden in itself. One full flower in summer's hot green shade can be as enchanting as an acre of blooms in a more propitious season. The young leaves of spring cast no pleasing shadows on the grass, nor do they whisper constantly as summer trees do. Winter, like summer, is a static season, but it is spare and skeletal. Summer's contours are lush and full; it is the full, the ripe, the restful season.

Colorful displays are unusual in summer, for the blooming season of ninety percent of the shrubs and bulbous plants hardy in the northern hemisphere is spring. However, summer can be made more colorful by assembling those few plants which are at once permanent, suitable for landscape planting, and colorful in summer, and placing them as advantageously as possible. This involves a botanist's knowledge, a horticulturist's practical skill, and an artist's sense of color and design. At Winterthur, several areas are skillfully designed to give a maximum amount of summer color: patches of woodland, blue in July with close-crowding spikes of the old-fashioned plantain-lily, *Hosta ventricosa;* hillsides bright with hawkweed, butterflyweed, and other native wildflowers; drifts of late-blooming rarities like the blazing red, plumleaf azalea *(Rhododendron prunifolium)* in July. But, bright as all these are, they cannot rival the displays of spring. For spring flowers have little competition except with each other; summer flowers compete with the whole landscape.

It is said that before the white man came, eastern North America was so heavily forested that a squirrel could travel from the Atlantic Ocean to the Mississippi River and never once touch the ground. Such forests must have been awe-inspiring, and we must note with regret the tiny remnant of them that now remains. But they must also have been a bit monotonous at times. Variety in the landscape is a marvelous thing, as in Japan where a few square miles may encompass a dozen types of terrain.

The wide open spaces of grasslands have quite as much appeal as forests, and it is

Cardinalflower. *Lobelia cardinalis*

The Pinetum

occasionally pleasing to have an unimpeded view of the sky. At Winterthur, of course, there is much consciously contrived variety in the terrain—woodland, wooded hillsides and valleys, meadow, swamp and bog, rocky slopes and open grassland. Certain days in late summer that have a hint of fall in their high, sharp blue, cloud-studded skies, seem especially suited for the open spaces. A skyscape needs something to tie it down, however, and nothing serves better than the pale spires of late hydrangeas *(H. paniculata)* and *Vitex.* The hydrangea, with long-lasting flowers of white turning to bronzy pink, and the vitex, with maple-like leaves, and spikes of blue, pink, or white flowers, are among the best of late shrubs. The "double" *Hydrangea paniculata,* the variety *grandiflora* (with all flowers in the cluster sterile), is the commonest form of this species. Blooming in late August, it is perhaps overplanted, but it is nevertheless a striking shrub or, if unpruned, a small tree. The typical form of the species, with clusters of mixed sterile and fertile flowers, is less common in gardens. It has a delicacy which is lacking in the commoner form, and is in my opinion more beautiful. Not to be overlooked is another variety, *tardiva,* which is similar to the ordinary type but begins blooming two or three weeks later, thus extending into autumn. *Vitex Agnus-castus,* one of the hardier woody members of the verbena family, *Verbenaceae,* is valued for its spikes of deep blue, pink, or white flowers in late summer. Near the northern limits of its range at Winterthur, it occasionally kills back during the winter, but nevertheless blooms on new growth the following summer. In the South, where it reaches the dimensions of a small tree, it is widely planted.

Expanses of water yield effects somewhat similar to those of open grasslands. In spring

August-Lilies on March Walk. *Hosta ventricosa*

P. G. Hydrangea. *H. paniculata grandiflora*

the pond is edged with wild forget-me-nots, a far-carrying pale blue in the green landscape. In late summer, the dying plants glow in the high August sun with a soft incandescence, while the still pond gives off a pale golden green reflection which lights up the leaves of the adjacent trees. An occasional fish may faintly stir the surface of the water, and a posturing heron may stand statue-like for long minutes at the water's edge. Even the normally active ducks and geese fly silently down to swim almost unnoticed near the shore.

Pond below Quarry

The somnolent mood of summer does not last long. Life quickens with the first touch of autumn. The herons vanish, and the far-off yelping of migrating geese sounds in the night. The native geese, too, begin flocking. Each morning they arrive, loud and boisterous now, as if enjoying the chilly breezes, to plunge on bowed wings from high in the sky and spend the day bathing in the ponds, grazing on the lawns, and gabbling contentedly in their melodious language.

Autumn

There is a day in August when autumn truly begins. In the morning there is a slight chill, and the sun that day will be high and pale and distant. It is not much more than a hint of things to come, so subtle that it passes almost unmarked by our consciousness. Soon the heat returns and summer moves on, but nothing is quite the same. We notice quite suddenly that whole limbs of the black gums have red leaves, that the dogwoods and shadbushes in the woods have a bronzed, burnished look. Telephone wires sag with great flocks of tree swallows. Blackbirds no longer travel in pairs but in polyglot bands of several species. Corn in the fields is in full ear and yellowing, and an occasional leaf on the sassafras is crimson. Winter is on its way.

Summer wanes into autumn, a time of continual movement, of high, clear skies and racing winds, falling leaves and the great migration of birds. Days of steady rain soak the earth, and days of steady wind dry it again. Leaves fall, spinning in the air, glinting gold in the shafts of sunlight that filter through the trees. From beech, ash, and hickory they rain down constantly for days, littering the ground with yellow, brown, and orange. The oaks turn late, becoming brown with touches of orange and red, but they retain their leaves, dry and dead, far into the winter.

Everywhere there are birds: flocks of grackles, redwings, cowbirds, and starlings swarming noisily across meadows and through treetops; bands of screaming jays; goldfinches, no longer yellow but olive, twittering and singing on the wing; cardinals flashing red among the evergreens; the ever-present sparrows; and, sure sign that summer has ended, wintry-voiced juncos in gray and white.

Lush September becomes brisk October, dreary November. Leaves fall endlessly, and suddenly stop. The vagabond blackbirds are one day seen perching on bare branches, and then they are gone. The movement of autumn slows, almost ceases. Nights are increasingly chill, morning landscapes are rimed with frost. During the day, drab sparrows move forlornly among the dead leaves and bare branches of the shrubbery. During the long nights, the cold descends almost like a living presence, gripping and pinching all things in its cruel grasp.

On the calendars of the ancients the year ended with autumn. And it really is an ending

"The William Penn Tree." Tulip-Tree or Tulip-Poplar. *Liriodendron tulipifera*

Rhododendron
mucronatum cv.
'Magnifica'

in the sense that it is a completion of the yearly cycle of growth and reproduction. With autumn, nature is finished for the year. But how magnificently she finishes!—with the clear blue of water and sky, the bronze of foliage, the flame of hawthorn, dogwood, and viburnum berry.

Now the trees, ignored in spring, gray ghosts of themselves in winter, come into their own in a vast color scheme of nature's devising. Pure yellow are the beeches and tulip-trees, bronze yellow the hickories and ashes. Maples are golden and orange red, black gums scarlet, sweet gums maroon and purple. The oaks are brownish, or bright red in some species.

The "William Penn Tree" in Chandler Woods, always magnificent, is even more so in autumn. In 1932, on the 250th anniversary of William Penn's arrival in Pennsylvania, a census was made in Pennsylvania, Delaware, and New Jersey of the trees which were probably growing when Penn sailed to Philadelphia. Some 250 trees were counted, and one of these, a tulip-poplar or tulip-tree *(Liriodendron tulipifera)* was found at Winterthur. Today it is immense, by far the biggest tree on the place, measuring almost seventeen feet in girth and towering well above one hundred feet.

Among autumn shrubs, the wild sweet-pepper bush, *Clethra alnifolia,* and the spice-bush, *Lindera Benzoin,* are outstanding for their clear yellow color. *Photinia villosa,* a small tree related to the apples which is naturalized at Winterthur, becomes a mixture of yellow, bronze, and clear pink, accented by clusters of glossy red berries. Dogwoods turn

Beech and Hickory near Pavilion Drive Pond

a rich wine color. The winged burning-bush, *Euonymus alatus,* one of the brightest of autumn shrubs, becomes a brilliant cherry red with cerise overtones. By the middle of October, autumn color is at its height. The leaves of dogwoods and redbuds are crimson and gold, the crimson of the dogwood's leaves contrasting almost violently with the pure scarlet of its berries. Azaleas are deep green, bronze, or mahogany. *R. mucronatum* cv. 'Magnifica' is further enhanced by large strawberry and white flowers.

Near the Quarry is a grove of *Idesia polycarpa:* tall, slender trees with large, tropical-looking leaves, laden with long, grapelike clusters of orange berries. Beneath the idesias, persimmons are covered with salmony orange fruits, callicarpas with violet, snowberries with white, *Poncirus trifoliata* with yellow, and *Viburnum setigerum* with coral red.

In the Pinetum several plants of *Pyracantha coccinea Lalandi* are great mounds of burnt orange now, in barbaric splendor against the steel blue of the junipers behind them. Elsewhere the leaves of the Korean rhododendron are a rich bronzy purple. The dawn redwood's foliage lies between straw yellow and copper. *Cotoneaster horizonatalis* and many of the Kurume-type azaleas are vinaceous purple and bronze over green.

Flowers produce the "atmosphere" of spring; foliage creates that of autumn. Autumn leaves set the landscape ablaze, falling leaves make constant movement, and fallen leaves, like snow, alter the visible world. The leaves give autumn one of its most distinctive sounds as they scurry and scrape across windblown roads, or crunch beneath the feet.

Foliage is not the whole of autumn. There are flowers, like the exquisite sasanqua camellias and their relative the beautiful franklinia, but these seem exotic, somehow out of tune with autumn. One feels intuitively that, with their lush flowering, they come from a region of no real winter and thus no real preparation for winter. The camellias, especially, seem the classic innocents of the plant world. As winter days approach, they bloom the more thickly, opening their large, delicate flowers to the harshest winds and the most killing frosts. The real autumn flowers are the crocuses and colchicums, which briefly lift their great purple goblets to the sun and then vanish, leaving the earth to winter.

Crocuses and colchicums are bulbous plants, and, like the vast majority of bulbs, have evolved in response to some factor in their environment which makes growth unfavorable during the summer months—either extreme summer aridity or excessive competition from other plants. They grow during the spring, when warm rains fall, and before larger plants leaf out and shade the ground—when growing conditions are, in other words, at the optimum. At the beginning of summer, their leaves wither, and they pass the unfavorable season in a dormant state, by means of an underground organ which contains stored food and water and the bud for next year's growth. They remain underground, protected from extremes of any kind, for perhaps nine months of the year, and it is therefore important that they make as much growth as possible during their short growing season; this growth determines the amount of food to be stored in the bulb for the following season. This is the main reason why the leaves of any bulb should never be removed until they have completely withered.

Most bulbs flower in the spring as, or even before, their leaves begin to grow. But a few send up only leaves in the spring, saving the flowers for autumn, when they rise magically, with no leaves and little warning, from the bare ground. These bulbs are valuable for the last splash of color in the garden. Perhaps the best known of these are members of the genus *Colchicum,* which comprises over twenty-five species native in Europe, Asia, and Asia Minor. Most colchicums have flowers of purple, lavender, mauve, or white. The only yellow species, *C. luteum,* is spring-flowering, difficult to grow, and reputedly "more curious than beautiful." Common in cultivation are only three or four species and a handful of hybrids, but these are among the most robust and beautiful in the genus. *Colchicum autumnale,* which because of its mauve-pink, leafless flowers is called "naked

Colchicum Hybrid

ladies" in England, is the first to flower, appearing early in September. Its widely opened flowers are reminiscent of waterlilies. *Colchicum giganteum, C.speciosum,* and *C.byzantinum* have larger mauve flowers, globular or tulip-shaped, and bloom in the middle of September. *Colchicum autumnale* has double forms in both mauve and white, and *C.speciosum* has a large white form which is very beautiful. Native to the mountains around the Mediterranean are several colchicums with flowers of purple and white arranged in a checkerboard pattern. These are strikingly exotic but, unfortunately, difficult to grow in most gardens. Much easier are the hybrids between the checkered species and *C.giganteum* and *speciosum. C.* cv. 'Violet Queen' is one of the earliest blooming of these, with large, white-throated mauve cups. Actually, these flowers are white, heavily checkered with mauve except in the throat. Another hybrid, 'Lilac Wonder,' has flowers of warm mauve with very pointed petals, and still another, 'The Giant,' has immense globular flowers of pinkish lavender with white throats.

Colchicums are often erroneously called autumn crocuses. They are similar to crocuses, though considerably larger, but the similarity is purely superficial. Crocuses belong to the iris family, colchicums to the lily family, and, like all liliaceous plants, have a whorl of six stamens in the throat of each flower. Members of the iris family have only three stamens. Even more revealing are the leaves of colchicums which, instead of being basal, narrow, and grasslike like those of crocuses, are lush and lilylike, on stems a foot or more tall. A lesson may be drawn from this difference: crocuses of all types are suitable

White Autumn Crocus. *Crocus speciosus albus*

for planting in lawns because the leaves lie so flat that only the lowest setting of a lawn-mower will cut them off. Colchicums will not persist in areas that are mowed in spring, any more than will lilies or tulips. They are only suited, then, to those sections of the garden that can be left untouched by the mower until early summer. The leaves of col-chicums sprout very early in the spring, and are quite handsome except for a brief period in June when they turn yellow and wither away. They do not appear again until the following spring. The huge bulbs (technically not true bulbs, but corms) are white, coated with a dark brown papery tunic. They look like oversized and misshapen tulip bulbs. Their dormant season—summer—is the best time to plant them, though they may also be planted in autumn. It is not unusual for fall-planted bulbs to flower a few days after they are placed in the ground. The colchicum bulb will in fact flower—once and no more—at its appointed time, whether it is planted or not; this characteristic has caused its pro-motion as a "wonder bulb" by dime stores, where in September it can often be seen sitting unplanted but in full flower on a bare counter.

Like most bulbous plants, colchicums look best in large quantities. Few sights are more charming than a whole hillside clothed in the soft lavender of colchicum. However, if one lacks the means to plant whole hillsides, a few plants tucked at the base of a tree or among shrubs make pleasing accents in fall. The culture of colchicums is very simple. Their only requirements are sun, or shade that is not too dense, and a chance to ripen their leaves completely in spring.

The scientific name of the plant derives from Colchis, the ancient country in Asia Minor where Jason sought the Golden Fleece. Scholars have long speculated about the identity

"Fall Daffodil."
Sternbergia lutea

of the Golden Fleece, and some modern ornithologists are convinced that what the Argonauts really brought to Greece was *Phasianus colchicus,* the metallically brilliant Colchis pheasant. The natural history of the Bible has been similarly studied, and has yielded some interesting results. For example, the "lily of the valley" and the "lily among thorns" were not the plants we know by these names today, but rather the hyancinth, *Hyacinthus orientalis.* The "rose of Sharon" was probably *Narcissus tazetta,* the paperwhite narcissus, which still covers the dry plains of Sharon. Neither the ancient writers nor their medieval and Elizabethan translators had the binomial system of Linnaeus to aid them in classifying plants, and hence the confusion of names.

A plant which, along with the anemones of the Palestinian hills, has been thought by many to be the biblical "lilies of the field" is *Sternbergia lutea.* This is a graceful plant, growing from a true bulb, with cup-shaped flowers of glistening yellow in September. It is a member of the amaryllis family and is often called the "fall daffodil," for it resembles its relatives, the narcissi, in leaf, stem, and flower. It does not, however, possess the trumpet or corona which makes the daffodil so distinctive. Unlike most other autumn-blooming bulbs, *Sternbergia lutea* sends up leaves along with its flowers. These remain green through the winter and early spring, and in cold climates are likely to be injured unless covered by a blanket of snow during cold snaps. In Delaware, the plant survives occasional drops to zero weather. It is not so robust as *Colchicum,* and does best in prepared beds or among shrubbery where it does not have too much competition from tall grass and vigorous

Bed of Colchicum

perennials. Another species, *S. Clusiana (S. macrantha)*, has somewhat larger, later flowers which appear before the leaves. Although *S. lutea* is readily procurable from bulb dealers, *S. Clusiana* is rare in the United States. Sternbergias should be planted during their dormant period in summer, and set four to six inches deep, in soil that is not overly moist. They seem to thrive in regions of hot summers, which is natural since they are native to the arid Middle East. The name commemorates Count Kaspar von Sternberg, a German botanist.

Third in this triumvirate of showy autumn bulbs is *Crocus*, the genus which provides so many wonderful additions to the spring garden. Everyone knows the spring crocuses. But few people bother with the autumn-blooming species, and this is a pity, for they are among the most beautiful of bulbs. Native for the most part to the dry regions of the Middle East, all they require in American gardens is a well drained soil and a certain amount of sun each day. Otherwise they thrive on neglect.

There are well over a dozen species of autumn crocuses. All are smaller than colchicums but larger than spring crocuses, with flowers borne on longer stems—actually not stems at all, but the elongated tubes of the flowers. Aside from their blooming season, they are much like their better known kin. They have the same narrow, grasslike leaves, green with a white midrib, which appear in early spring and die down in June. Their corms are almost indistinguishable from those of spring-blooming crocuses. Since their fragile flowers are likely to be obscured by long grass, it is well to plant them in lawns where the grass is kept short in summer, or among shrubs or perennial plants where the ground is cultivated. Summer cultivation does not in the least bother them, and in fact seems to aid in spreading the tiny cormels which form around the main corm. The corms of autumn crocuses should be planted in late summer and early fall. Their blooming season is a bit later than that of the colchicums—late September and early October. Like colchicums, they will sometimes flower on schedule even if left out of the ground, though this is a great strain on them. If corms are received late in the season, however, those that have not flowered will be likely to do so within a few days after planting, and the others will quickly establish themselves for the following year. They should be planted three inches deep in a sunny or partially shaded, well drained location.

The commonest and, surprisingly (for the most easily pleased species is too often the least beautiful), one of the best of the autumn crocuses is *Crocus speciosus*, from eastern Europe and Asia Minor. It grows to about four inches in height, and in its typical form is a soft mauve blue, much bluer than any of the colchicums. The variant called 'Oxonian' is almost a true deep blue, and *albus* is a delicately beautiful white form of the species. *C. speciosus* is perhaps the most easily obtained of the autumn crocuses. Another that is equally beautiful and almost as easy to obtain is *C. Kotschyanus*. It is like *speciosus* in form, but soft lavender in color, its throat zoned with bright orange; it is usually listed in catalogues as *C. zonatus*. The stigmata of these two species, like those of the spring crocuses, are a brilliant red orange and seem to leap from the cool cups of the flowers like little tongues of flame. Another autumn species, the saffron crocus *(C. sativus)*, has stigmata so long that they protrude even from the closed flowers. These are still harvested in the Mediterranean region for the valuable flavoring substance called saffron. It is said that about four thousand stigmata are required to produce one ounce of saffron. The species, which has large mauve flowers, is beautiful as well as valuable, and well worth a place in the garden. The name crocus, incidentally, comes from the ancient Greek word for saffron.

Several other species of autumn crocuses exist, but few are available in the trade. One is worthy of mention for its distinctive qualities: *C. byzantinus*, not to be confused with *Colchicum byzantinum* (as *Crocus speciosus* is not to be confused with *Colchicum speciosum*).

Lilyturf. *Liriope Muscari*

A woodland plant native in eastern Europe, *C. byzantinus* possesses flowers of deep purple blue which consist of three large outer and three small inner segments, so that the flower resembles a tiny iris as much as a crocus. So distinct is it that one botanist has devised a new genus for it, *Crociris*. Most crocuses have orange stigmata, but those of this species are extremely feathery and bright purplish blue in color. It is a rare plant, unusual and interesting, and unlike most other autumn crocuses, seems to do better in shade than in sun.

From Asia comes a group of plants which appear to be intermediate between grasses and grape hyacinths. Their flowers, white or more often some shade of violet, and borne on erect spikes, are definitely liliaceous, but their linear leaves and tufted, clumped manner of growth are almost indistinguishable from many grasses. Their common name is, appropriately, "lilyturf," and they fall botanically into two related genera: *Ophiopogon* and *Liriope*. By far the commonest in American gardens, and perhaps the best suited, is *Liriope Muscari,* a clump-forming plant with dark, glossy, evergreen leaves and bright lilac flowers in August and September, followed by black berries. The variety *variegata* has leaves which are longitudinally striped with cream white, and the form called 'Monroe White' has green leaves and white flowers. Liriope, a nymph of classical mythology, was the mother of Narcissus; *Muscari,* the botanical name of the grape hyacinth, refers to the flowers. It is consistently confused with another lilyturf, *Ophiopogon Jaburan,* which is very similar but has less showy, white flowers. There are several other lilyturfs available, especially in the South. One of the best is the Japanese "mondo-grass," *Ophiopogon japonicus,* a dwarf, mat-forming species with black-green leaves and pale lavender flowers. Lilyturfs belong to the lily family.

All the lilyturfs mentioned are hardy in the East as far north as New York City, but since they have evergreen leaves, they do better when planted in sheltered locations and when given some form of winter protection in the northern portion of their range. Cold winter winds soon kill the leaves and destroy their effectiveness. But this seems not to affect the plants adversely, and in spring they send up new leaves.

As ground cover, lilyturfs are superb, especially for shady spots where grass cannot be induced to grow. As rather formal edgings along walks and on the borders of flowerbeds, they are also excellent. Most do not spread rapidly, but form tight clumps of leaves. If rapid increase is desired, these clumps may be divided into single pieces each year. *Liriope Muscari* makes an elegant accent plant, which is pleasing all the year round, and especially showy when in bloom. Its variegated form is most striking as an accent, although, like all plants with variegated foliage, it must be used with some discretion.

Before autumn leaves begin to take on their color there is a period of stasis. It is a restful period, when wet meadows and pastures are covered with the best of the late summer flowers—lemon yellow sneezeweed; pale cone-flowers; mauve, blue, blue-gray, and white asters; blue and white vervains and eupatoriums; purple gerardias; and rich maroon ironweed. Even the flowers that have passed add color to the scene: thistles and lowly dandelions are tipped by cottony puffs of seed heads; tall panic and red-top grasses are graceful and bright with spikes of seed; tulip-trees carry upright, pale, conelike fruits among their leaves; sweet gums dangle their strange spikey globes; oaks drop their windfall of rich, polished brown acorns.

As autumn progresses, color appears in unexpected quarters. The lily-of-the-valley bears its winsome and fragrant flowers in spring, and is usually associated with spring in our minds (even its scientific name, *Convallaria majalis,* which may be roughly translated "in the valleys of May," alludes to spring), yet its racemes of large red berries are handsome, making a planting of *Convallaria* as attractive in autumn as it is in spring. Many woodland plants have showy fruits. False solomonseal bears a kind of plume of orange-red

Lilyturf in Pool Garden

Fruits of Umbrella Tree.
Magnolia tripetala

berries. Jack-in-the-pulpit lifts up a dense cluster of brilliant scarlet fruits. Wild spikenard and baneberries are more handsome in fruit than in flower. Even the roses bear colorful hips, from the pea-sized fruits of *Rosa multiflora* to the elegant flagon-shaped hips of *Rosa Moyesii*.

The genus *Magnolia* is associated with some of the most opulent flowers in the plant kingdom, yet all the magnolias also bear attractive fruits, and one species, the cucumber-tree *(Magnolia acuminata)*, has fruits which are at least as showy as its flowers. All magnolia fruits are fleshy and roughly cylindrical in shape. Those of the Asiatic species are asymmetrical for the most part, shaped rather like small, twisted bananas, while those of the American species are symmetrical and larger—the shape and sometimes the size of cucumbers. In color they are bright rose, and when fully ripe they split at regular intervals along their surfaces, exposing brilliant orange seeds which gradually emerge from rapidly drying fruits and dangle on short filaments.

Of the dozen or so magnolias at Winterthur, only a few are hardy and vigorous enough to establish themselves in the woodlands. Two species, both American and both established in the woodlands at Winterthur, are worth growing for fruit alone. These, the umbrella-tree *(Magnolia tripetala)* and the bigleaf magnolia *(M. macrophylla)*, are robust trees with huge leaves. The bigleaf magnolia has the largest leaves and flowers of any hardy magnolia: its leaves are sometimes three feet long, and its flowers, appearing in midsummer, are dinner-plate size, some fourteen inches across. Needless to say, this is not a tree for a small front yard, but it is excellent where a bold or even overpowering effect is desired. *M. macrophylla* is deciduous, and in fall it bears many large pink fruits.

M. tripetala is not quite so overpowering, though still too bold and tropical in appearance to fit into the small landscape. Its leaves occasionally reach two feet in length, and because they tend to cluster at the branch tips (hence its common name), they produce a palmlike or banana-like effect. The ivory flowers are smaller than those of *M. macrophylla* and appear in late May. They have a strong scent which some people find attractive. In fall the pale green leaves turn a wonderful mahogany bronze, and for a brief period have the color and texture of fine morocco leather. The fruits are perhaps the showiest in the genus—large, bright rose, and borne in abundance at the tips of the heavy branches. They produce a fine autumn effect before they become food for hungry migrating birds.

Whether in the cultivated sections of the garden or in the untouched depths of the woods, the trees are first to announce autumn. In August the sun begins perceptibly to wane; its light grows paler and more diffuse. Soon the leaves of the trees seem to grow paler also, and cast less definite patterns of light and darkness beneath them. In the early summer woodland there are true contrasts between sun and shadow. One passes from hot, brilliant patches of sun into cool, dark areas of shade; the sun is high and bright, the foliage of the trees dense and heavy. But in late summer, the lowering sun passes through the leaves at another angle. The trees seem to have thinned out, and the diffused light striking the ground seems almost chill.

By this time, all that can be said about the joys of summer has been said by the ovenbird. His incredibly loud voice has reverberated from tree to tree, swelled in the damp shade of laurel thickets, and shattered the silence of a hot dusty road. His song issues from his tiny throat like the tolling of a great bell, louder and louder, until its sheer volume becomes exquisitely unbearable. And when he has stopped, as suddenly as he began, an echo rings in one's ears for long minutes afterwards. In the dead of winter, I can hear the voice of the ovenbird ringing through Chandler Woods.

By November nearly all the leaves will have fallen. Even those of the Turkey oak and the linden viburnum, which remain green until the first frost, will now hang dejectedly, black and crumpled, from the branches.

This is the time when we first taste the grimness of winter. All of nature seems forlorn and naked. But there are occasional delights. One of these is *Galanthus corcyrensis*, a long-stemmed snowdrop with all the grace and purity of its spring-flowering kin. Another, the native witch-hazel, *Hamamelis virginiana*, now is covered with spidery, straw yellow blossoms. It is not as showy as its oriental relatives, but it blooms in a bleak season, when it seems we ought not even hope for flowers. Colorful too at this late season are the leaves of plants which are classified as "semi-evergreen"—plants whose leaves will be retained until the coldest days of winter. Typical is the hybrid *Viburnum × Burkwoodi*, which has as one parent the deciduous *V. Carlesii* and as the other, the evergreen *V. utile*. The Burkwood viburnum always seems to be in conflict as winter approaches. In September and October, the leaves of occasional branches will suddenly turn flaming scarlet in contrast to the shining dark green leaves of the rest of the plant; as autumn progresses, leaves here and there turn yellow, red, or pinkish orange and drop, while others remain green into the depths of winter. It is as if the plant could not make up its mind how to deal with the season. Less confused but also less entertaining are the "evergreen" azaleas, which keep only part of their leaves through the winter, usually a rich, vinaceous bronze in color; and the jetbead, *Rhodotypus scandens*, whose leaves seem to bleach rather than change color as autumn progresses, fading slowly to the very palest shade of green, then to an ivory white before dropping late in the season.

The jetbead is one of those virtuous but unassuming plants which are too often passed

Autumn Trees

by in favor of gaudier plant material. In late spring, and sporadically through the summer, it produces white flowers similar to single roses, and in autumn, each arching twig and branch terminates in a cluster of four hard, dry seeds, shining and jet black in color. The plant is therefore interesting throughout much of the year.

The main source of color during the bleak period of late autumn is neither flowers nor foliage, but fruit. This is the time when berried trees and shrubs come into their own: callicarpa, with berries of an unbelievably intense violet; scarlet and crimson hawthorn; glistening red viburnum; glacier white snowberry; oriental persimmon with large globes of gaudy orange; the *Poncirus trifoliata*, the only hardy citrus species, with velvety yellow balls like miniature grapefruits.

Plants with showy fruits have an adorned, bejeweled quality that is lacking in flowering plants. They give one a feeling of richness and ripeness that is the essence of autumn, Keats's "season of mellow fruitfulness." On these days after the first frost, when the few leaves left on the trees have a crisped, pinched, burned look, and when a sharp burrlike smoke fills the cold air, the birds come in flocks to sample the fruit: smart cedar waxwings

Chandler Woods

with sleek seal-brown feathers and bandit-masked eyes, who love most of all the tiny sour crab apples; starlings, metamorphosed from mere black birds to splendid fellows in metallic green, stippled from bill to tail-tip with white dots like constellations of stars, who, with their too-knowing, too-intelligent eyes, like and eat everything. The mockingbird comes too, buoyant and mothlike on his white-spotted wings, and may be joined by the season's last forlorn robin. All these birds deplete the berries, of course, but time would dispose of them in any case. And in exchange for the berries we have the never-ending amusement provided by the birds.

In spite of birds and the elements, many berry-bearing trees and shrubs are colorful for an amazingly long time. Most flowering shrubs, in fact, are evanescent in comparison. The lacquered red berries of the linden viburnum *(Viburnum dilatatum)*, for example, shine among deep green foliage in October and continue to light up the black branches in late December, long after the leaves have fallen. Equally beautiful is the tea viburnum *(V. setigerum)*, one of the finest plants to be introduced into cultivation in recent years. With its vase-shaped habit, arching branches, and long, pointed leaves, it is one of the most elegant plants available. And the berries, deep coral red (orange in the variety *aurantiacum*) in heavy, drooping clusters, make it one of the most spectacular viburnums in fruit.

Many other viburnums are worth growing for autumn fruits. *Viburnum dilatatum xanthocarpum* is a variety of the linden viburnum, with berries of a lovely primrose yellow. The American cranberry-bush, *V. trilobum*, has maple-like leaves and pretty white flowers,

Snowberries.
Symphoricarpos albus

followed in autumn by showy, red, acid fruits which are excellent in tart jellies and sauces. Another native with edible fruits and ornamental qualities is the black-haw, *V. prunifolium;* its berries, quickly eaten by birds, are dark blue. Finally, we have *V. nudum,* the smooth withe-rod, a most beautiful species that is consistently ignored by gardeners and professional plantsmen alike. It has leathery, shining, deep green leaves which turn a rich burgundy in the autumn. In June it bears flat heads of creamy flowers which ripen slowly into clusters of large, oval berries. These are at first green, turning in succession to white, bright pink, and finally blue. The berries ripen erratically, and the resulting multicolored clusters of white, pink, and blue are extremely striking. *Viburnum nudum* is native in damp woods from New York to Florida.

For berries of unusual coloring, few plants can equal the beauty-berries, *Callicarpa.* All the species in the genus bear small but abundant clusters of rich lilac or violet berries in late October and November. These are handsome in combination with the pale yellow flowers of the American witch-hazel *(Hamamelis virginiana),* which blooms in November. Perhaps the brightest blue in nature is found in the fruits of *Symplocos paniculata,* the sapphire-berry. This plant has no drawbacks. A small tree at maturity, it is well suited for modest gardens. In spring it is attractive with its frothy white flowers, and in September, when its rich china blue berries begin to ripen, it is truly magnificent.

In the United States, we make little use of our native persimmon, *Diospyros virginiana.* The people of the Orient, in contrast, have developed their species *(D. Kaki)* into a fruit of

Firethorn. *Pyracantha coccinea Lalandi*

Oriental Persimmon.
Diospyros Kaki

great commercial importance. Most varieties of oriental persimmon have fruits the size and shape of a peach, bright orange in color, and delightful to look at. The palatability of persimmons seems to be a matter of individual taste. They are the least acid of any fruits, having when unripe an odd, astringent, but non-acid quality that puckers the mouth most unpleasantly, and, when ripe, a honeyed sweetness that some find too cloying. Taste aside, the oriental persimmon is worth growing for purely ornamental reasons, for when hung with its great orange globes in autumn, it is truly spectacular.

But perhaps the most pleasing of all the fruits of autumn are those of the flowering quinces *(Chaenomeles)*, which are a bonus. The flowering quince is grown primarily for its brilliant spring flowers. The fruit, however, is not only handsome but highly edible, producing a clear, amber, pectin-rich juice which makes a delicate and delicious jelly. Furthermore, they are the most fragrant fruits I know, perfuming the air as strongly as any flower. The Chaenomeles Walk in the Pinetum is delightful in September and October, when all the bushes are laden with the large yellowish green fruits, like asymmetrical apples, among which an occasional out-of-season flower shines. As the distant autumn sun warms the air, a spicy musk rises from the fruits, and wafts through the Pinetum, a fragrance rich and strange, heady and satisfying. It is to the nostrils what the yellow and red woodlands are to the eyes, and what the sounds of migrating birds and swirling leaves are to the ears—the abundant completion of autumn.

All too soon the bright side of autumn is eclipsed. Eventually no colorful leaves are left

Fruits of Flowering Quince. *Chaenomeles*

to fall. Hungry birds have decimated the brilliant berries. The wind changes from brisk to bitter. Fallen leaves, their color lost, lie lifeless and brown, already crumbling to dust. The most typical sound of this period is the dismal and monotonous rasping of lawn rakes.

Now, as the globe, spinning toward the winter solstice, inclines its northern hemisphere farther and farther away from the sun, the long dark nights of winter overtake us. Ice closes the ponds; even the geese forsake us. Oppressed by cold and darkness, by the bareness of winter trees, we find cheer only occasionally—in the changeless forms of evergreens, in the bright red and green of the holly. This is a quiet time, a time of waiting.

One day a wan sun appears in the milky sky, but sheds no warmth. A cold light, pale, almost unreal, is cast over the garden. There is an unnatural stillness everywhere. The sparrows are silent but agitated, quickened into movement, assiduously gleaning food from the barren woods and fields as though they know time is short. Before nightfall the snow begins, the first of the season, in tiny flakes at first, then larger, heavy and wet. The snow, as it gains momentum, falls on a strangely hushed world. There is no movement but that of the white flakes slanting down from the dark sky, no sound but that of the cold wind sweeping through the trees.

The following day, the sun rises on an earth transformed, a still, unravished landscape of dazzling white. Winter has come, and even with its coming has brought the seeds of spring. For the winter snow is a great insulating blanket, locking in the rising heat of the earth, and locking out the penetrating frost and the ice-laden winds from the north. If you were to dig a daffodil bulb now, you would find that already it has long, tender white roots growing into the soil around it and pale leaf-spears extending up towards the surface of the ground. The snow covers a world that is dead only on the surface. Deep in the ground, and deep in the living tissues of plants, preparation is slowly being made for spring. The circle of the year closes with its beginning.

First Snow on March Walk

Author's Note

Because this book is not a botanical handbook, I have considered it unnecessary to follow strict rules of botanical nomenclature in the citation of the author's name following mention of each species. For example, it is assumed that *Acer rubrum* is the maple species named by Linnaeus (that is, the species currently accepted by the International Code of Botanical Nomenclature as *A. rubrum*) rather than that named by Lamarck (which is known under the Botanical Code as *A. saccharinum*). In most cases, text and photographs clearly identify the plant in question.

I have rejected the current horticultural practice of writing all specific names in lower-case letters as a practice which confuses more than it simplifies. There is precedent in English for the capitalization of proper nouns, and it follows that species names derived from them (such as *Smithii, Juddii,* and *Sieboldii*) should also be capitalized. More important, the capitalization of old generic names or native names should be retained as an aid to understanding the rules of botanical nomenclature. The serious student will recognize that the gender of the Latin noun *Acer* is neuter because the majority of the specific epithets in this genus carry the Latin neuter ending "-um." But what will he do when he sees combinations like *Acer pseudo-platanus,* which apparently carries the Latin masculine ending "-us," or *Acer negundo,* which carries no recognizable ending at all? *Acer Pseudo-platanus,* on the other hand, tells him that the specific epithet is either a pre-Linnaean or an aboriginal name for the sycamore maple of Europe (in this case the former), and *Acer Negundo* tells him the same thing, in this case the latter, *Negundo* being the Indian name for the American box-elder.

For the most part, common names have been used in this book in preference to scientific names, except where, for purposes of identification, both have been given. The great difficulty here is that acceptable common names are sometimes hard to find. Some plants, such as jack-in-the-pulpit, have dozens of common names, and others have none at all. The situation is further confused by the fact that some common names apply to several different plants. "Bluebell," for instance, can be either a squill *(Scilla),* a bellflower *(Campanula),* or a borage *(Mertensia).* When the only alternative is a semi-barbarous coinage or insipid translation of the Latin, I prefer using the scientific name as the common name. Such practice gives us chrysanthemum, zinnia, petunia, althea, gladiolus, iris, and a host of others which usage has made common. "Chrysanthemum," for example, is far more explicit than its literal translation, "gold-flower."

In current horticultural practice the abbreviation *cv.* ("cultivar" or "cultivated variety") is often used to indicate named varieties of plants developed *in cultivation (Rose cv. 'Coral Creeper')* as opposed to botanical varieties of plants *(Ranunculus repens villosus)* developing spontaneously in the wild. The term has no botanical significance, and its use depends strictly on one's own discretion.

Wherever possible, I have attempted to give some information on the hardiness of the plants described in this book. The zoning system given below is that used by the Arnold Arboretum. Figures are in Fahrenheit, and indicate the *average* minimum temperatures for each zone. Winterthur lies in the southern half of Zone 6.

ZONE 1: Northern Canada, beyond the line of permafrost.

ZONE 2: −50 to −35 degrees. Canada, northern North Dakota, Minnesota, Montana.

ZONE 3: −35 to −20 degrees. Northern New England, North Central states, high-elevation Rocky Mountain states.

ZONE 4: −20 to −10 degrees. Most of New England, New York, Great Lakes Region, Central Plains states, Rocky Mountains.

ZONE 5: −10 to −5 degrees. Southern New England, Pennsylvania, Ohio, southern Indiana, southern Illinois, Missouri, southern Kansas, much of the Southwest.

ZONE 6: −5 to +5 degrees. Cape Cod, New Jersey, northern Delaware, Maryland, Appalachia, northern Arkansas and Oklahoma.

ZONE 7: 5 to 10 degrees. Southern New Jersey, southern Delaware and Maryland, central Virginia, Southern Mountain states, central Texas.

ZONE 8: 10 to 20 degrees. Coastal Virginia, inland South and Gulf states, southern Texas, southern Arizona, Sierra-Cascade regions of Pacific states.

ZONE 9: 20 to 30 degrees. Coastal North Carolina and South Carolina, coastal Georgia, most of Florida, coastal Gulf states and Texas, and coastal regions of Washington, Oregon, and northern California.

ZONE 10: 30 to 40 degrees. Southern half of Florida and southern coastal California.

Index

Illustrations are indicated by page numbers in italics.

DESIGN BY ULRICH RUCHTI